The Calendar of Minds

ADITI SINGH

Where reality meets expectations and mental health meets self discovery

Paperback ISBN 979-8-89906-646-7

Hardcase ISBN 979-8-89929-314-6

To Dr. Pritesh Gautam

I would like to extend my deepest gratitude to Dr. Pritesh Gautam, a remarkable individual who has dedicated his life to healing the unseen wounds of the mind.

Your tireless efforts to support those struggling with mental health issues have not gone unnoticed. Your kindness, compassion, and expertise have made a profound impact on the lives of countless individuals, including my own.

I am forever grateful for the guidance and support you provided me during the most challenging times of my life. Your unwavering dedication to your patients is a testament to your exceptional character and commitment to your craft.

Thank you for being a beacon of hope and healing in a world where mental health support is often needed but not always accessible. Your work is a reminder that even the most unseen wounds can be healed with the right care and compassion.

Once again, I express my heartfelt thanks for all that you do. Your selfless service to humanity is a blessing, and I feel fortunate to have had the opportunity to benefit from your expertise.

May your remarkable work continue to inspire and heal those who need it most.

Sincerely,

Aditi

Contents

This book takes you on a journey of self-discovery and growth, with each chapter representing a month of the year. From setting expectations in January to reflecting on the beginning, middle, and end in December, this book guides you through the ups and downs of life, offering valuable lessons and insights along the way.

About the Book

Chapter 1: January - The Month of Expectations

January marks the beginning of a new year, filled with possibilities and promise. This chapter explores the theme of expectations, encouraging readers to reflect on their goals, aspirations, and what they hope to achieve in the coming year. By setting clear expectations, readers can establish a foundation for personal growth and self-discovery.

Chapter 2: February - The Month of Reflections

February invites readers to slow down and reflect on their experiences, relationships, and choices. This chapter delves into the importance of introspection, self-awareness, and acknowledging areas for improvement. By examining their thoughts, emotions, and actions, readers can gain valuable insights and develop a deeper understanding of themselves.

Chapter 3: March - A Month of Hope

March represents a time of renewal and rebirth, as winter's chill begins to fade. This chapter focuses on the theme of hope, exploring its role in overcoming adversity, building resilience, and cultivating a positive mindset. Readers will discover how hope can serve as a powerful catalyst for personal growth and transformation.

Chapter 4: The April Awakening

April's arrival signals a time of awakening, as the world around us bursts forth in vibrant colors and new life. This chapter explores the concept of awakening, encouraging readers to shake off complacency and embrace change. By letting go of limiting beliefs and embracing their true potential, readers can experience a profound sense of renewal and rebirth.

Chapter 5: May - The Month of Letting Go

May's theme revolves around the art of letting go, releasing attachment to things that no longer serve us. This chapter guides readers in identifying areas where they may be holding on too tightly, whether it's a toxic relationship, a negative mindset, or a stagnant situation. By learning to release and surrender, readers can create space for new experiences, relationships, and opportunities.

Chapter 6: June - The Month of Authenticity

June celebrates the theme of authenticity, encouraging readers to embrace their true selves, without apology or pretension. This chapter explores the importance of living authentically, being true to one's values, passions, and desires. By embracing their authentic selves, readers can experience a deeper sense of freedom, confidence, and fulfillment.

Chapter 7: July - The Month of Kindness

July's theme focuses on the transformative power of kindness, exploring its impact on ourselves and those around us. This chapter guides readers in cultivating kindness, empathy, and compassion, and discovering the profound effects these qualities can have on our well-being and relationships.

Chapter 8: August - The Month of Emotional Freedom

August's theme revolves around the concept of emotional freedom, encouraging readers to release emotional burdens and cultivate a deeper sense of emotional intelligence. This chapter explores the importance of acknowledging, accepting, and expressing emotions in a healthy, constructive manner, leading to greater emotional freedom and resilience.

Chapter 9: Quantum Leap September - Embracing Sudden Transformation

September marks a turning point in the book, as readers are invited to embrace sudden transformation and quantum leaps in their personal growth journey. This chapter explores the concept of rapid transformation, encouraging readers to be open to new experiences, perspectives, and opportunities that can propel them forward in their journey.

Chapter 10: October - Learning the Art of Pouring Your Own Cup

October's theme focuses on the importance of self-care and prioritizing one's own needs. This chapter guides readers in learning the art of pouring their own cup, filling themselves up with love, care, and compassion, rather than relying on external sources. By prioritizing self-care, readers can experience greater resilience, confidence, and overall well-being.

Chapter 11: November - The Month of Attitude of Gratitude - Shifting Your Focus to the Good

November's theme celebrates the power of gratitude, encouraging readers to shift their focus to the good things in their lives. This chapter explores the transformative effects of gratitude on mental health, relationships, and overall well-being, guiding readers in cultivating a consistent practice of gratitude.

Chapter 12: December - The Beginning, Middle, and End

December's theme invites readers to reflect on their journey, acknowledging the beginning, middle, and end of their personal growth journey. This chapter encourages readers to integrate the lessons and insights gained throughout the book, embracing the cyclical nature of growth and transformation. By acknowledging the beginning, middle, and end, readers can experience a deeper sense of closure, renewal, and preparation for the new year ahead.

Prologue

Where Reality Meets Expectations and Mental Health Meets Self-Discovery

As we embark on this journey of self-discovery, we find ourselves at the intersection of two profound themes: the convergence of reality and expectations, and the intricate dance between mental health and self-discovery.

The Convergence of Reality and Expectations

We begin each new year with a sense of hope and optimism, filled with expectations of what the future holds. We set goals, make resolutions, and envision the person we want to become. However, as the months unfold, reality often meets us with unexpected challenges, setbacks, and surprises.

This convergence of reality and expectations can be a powerful catalyst for growth, forcing us to confront our limitations, re-evaluate our priorities, and adapt to the ever-changing landscape of life. It is in these moments of tension between reality and expectations that we discover our greatest opportunities for self-discovery, learning, and transformation.

The Intersection of Mental Health and Self-Discovery

Mental health and self-discovery are intimately intertwined, each informing and influencing the other. As we navigate the complexities of life, our mental health is constantly evolving, shaped by our experiences, relationships, and choices.

Self-discovery, in turn, is the process of exploring our thoughts, emotions, and behaviors, seeking to understand ourselves and our place in the world. This journey of self-discovery is deeply connected to our mental health, as it allows us to develop greater self-awareness, build resilience, and cultivate coping strategies for navigating life's challenges.

Embracing the Journey

As we embark on this journey of self-discovery, we are invited to embrace the complexities, challenges, and opportunities that lie ahead. We will explore the depths of our own hearts, minds, and spirits, cultivating the courage, resilience, and wisdom to navigate the twists and turns of life.

Through this journey, we will discover that reality and expectations are not mutually exclusive, but rather, they are intertwined aspects of our growth and transformation. We will learn to approach mental health and self-discovery as complementary facets of our overall well-being, fostering a deeper understanding of ourselves and our place in the world.

So come, join me on this journey of self-discovery, where reality meets expectations and mental health meets self-discovery. Let us explore, learn, and grow together, embracing the complexities and beauty of the human experience.

Dear Readers,

As you hold this book in your hands, I invite you to embark on a journey of self-discovery, growth, and transformation. Imagine that every character, every experience, and every emotion within these pages is a reflection of your own life. You are the protagonist, the hero, and the heart of this narrative.

Your well-being is paramount to me, and I hope that as we navigate the pages of this book together, you will come to understand the profound significance of prioritizing your mental health. It is a journey that requires courage, resilience, and compassion, but one that holds the promise of liberation, empowerment, and profound growth.

I acknowledge that I am not perfect, and that I may have stumbled along the way. But I am a learner, and I will always be open to growth, improvement, and the wisdom that comes from our shared human experiences.

As we walk this path together, I ask for your understanding, patience, and trust. Know that the characters and stories within these pages are fictional, yet born from the depths of my own heart and soul. They are a testament to the human spirit's capacity for resilience, hope, and transformation.

My intention is to support and guide you on your own path of self-discovery, to offer a comforting hand, a listening ear, and a reassuring voice that whispers, "You are not alone." I am committed to helping you in any way I can, and I invite you to reach out to me whenever you need support, guidance, or simply a reminder that you are seen, heard, and valued.

Let us join forces to create a ripple effect of positivity, compassion, and understanding that resonates across the globe. Together, we can break down stigmas, foster empathy, and cultivate a culture that celebrates the beauty, diversity, and complexity of the human experience.

Thank you for being part of this journey, for trusting me with your time, your energy, and your heart. I am honored to share my words, my heart, and my soul with you, and I look forward to walking alongside you on this path of self-discovery, growth, and transformation.

With love, compassion, and deepest gratitude,

Aditi

Chapter – 1

January: The Month of Expectations

"The greatest glory in living lies not in never falling, but in rising every time we fall."

- Nelson Mandela

Meet Aisha, a bright-eyed and ambitious 25-year-old who's bursting with excitement as she welcomes the new year. She's got a spring in her step and a sparkle in her eye, and she can't wait to dive headfirst into the next 12 months.

As she sips her morning coffee, Aisha pulls out her planner and begins to map out her vision for the year. She's got big plans, and she's determined to make them happen.

"Okay, let's see," she says to herself, "by December, I want to have taken two amazing trips, one to Kashmir and one to South. I want to have started a new job that I love, and I want to have saved up enough money to move into my own apartment. And, of course, I want to be rocking a fit and healthy body, thanks to regular gym workouts and a balanced diet."

Aisha's eyes shine with excitement as she writes down her goals. She can already imagine herself exploring the streets of Kerala, trying new foods in Kashmir, and feeling confident and strong in her own skin.

As she continues to plan, Aisha's list grows longer and more ambitious. She wants to learn a new language, take up a new hobby, and volunteer regularly. She wants to read more books, watch more movies, and spend quality time with her loved ones.

By the time she finishes writing, Aisha feels like she's on top of the world. She's got a clear plan, a positive attitude, and a sense of determination that's hard to shake.

"Bring it on, 2025!" she exclaims, pumping her fist in the air. "I'm ready for you!"

As Aisha dives into the new year, she's filled with a sense of possibility and promise. She knows that there will be ups and downs along the way, but she's ready to take on whatever comes her way.

And as she looks back on her planner, she can't help but feel a sense of pride and accomplishment. She's got a plan, and she's ready to make it happen.

The Energy of Expectation: A Cocktail of Hope and Dopamine

As we step into the new year, our minds are buzzing with excitement and anticipation. We've got big plans, and we're determined to make them happen. But what fuels this energy of expectation? What sparks the fire of hope within us?

The answer lies in our brain chemistry. When we set goals and imagine a brighter future, our brains release a cocktail of hormones that make us feel good. Dopamine, the neurotransmitter of pleasure and reward, is one of the key players. It's the hormone that makes us feel motivated, focused, and driven to achieve our dreams.

As the winter months wrap us in their cozy blanket, our bodies naturally crave comfort and relaxation. But amidst the snowflakes and hot chocolate, our minds are busy conjuring up visions of a dreamy life. We imagine ourselves succeeding, thriving, and living our best lives. And with each passing day, our expectations grow, fueled by the promise of a new year.

The energy of expectation is like a warm hug on a cold winter's night. It's the feeling of snuggling up by the fireplace, surrounded by loved ones, and knowing that everything is going to be alright. It's the sense of possibility that comes with a blank page, waiting to be filled with the stories of our lives.

As we bask in the glow of expectation, our minds become fertile ground for hope to take root. We start to believe in ourselves, our abilities, and our potential. We begin to see the world as a place of endless possibilities, where dreams can come true and miracles can happen.

Expectations

The whispered promises of a brighter tomorrow. The tantalizing hints of a life yet to be lived. Like the first blush of dawn on a summer morning, expectations paint the horizon with hues of possibility, beckoning us to step into the unknown.

In the tapestry of life, expectations are the vibrant threads that weave together the fabric of our dreams. They are the sparks that set our hearts aflame, illuminating the path ahead and guiding us through the twists and turns of our journey.

Just as the teenage years are a kaleidoscope of colors, a maelstrom of emotions, and a whirlwind of discovery, expectations are the kaleidoscope of our imagination, reflecting the ever-changing hues of our desires. Every experience, every encounter, every decision is a new shade, a new texture, a new dimension added to the rich tapestry of our lives.

In the teenage years, everything is new, everything is fresh, and every feeling is intense. The first love, the first heartbreak, the first triumph, and the first failure – each is a universe unto itself, a world of wonder, a world of discovery. And expectations are the stardust that sprinkles magic upon these experiences, making them shine with an otherworldly light.

Just as the teenager's heart beats faster with anticipation, expectations make our own hearts sing with promise. They are the whispered secrets of a life yet to be lived, the hidden messages of a future yet to be written. They are the possibilities that tantalize, the maybes that mesmerize, and the what-ifs that haunt us.

And yet, just as the teenage years are a time of growth, of exploration, and of self-discovery, expectations are a double-edged sword. They can be the wind beneath our wings, lifting us up to soar to great heights, or they can be the weights that anchor us to the ground, holding us back from realizing our true potential.

But even in their uncertainty, expectations are a reminder that life is a journey, not a destination. They are the whispers of a universe that is constantly unfolding, constantly evolving, and constantly surprising us. They are the hints of a tomorrow that is yet to be written, a tomorrow that is full of promise, full of possibility, and full of wonder.

So let us cherish expectations, these tantalizing whispers of a life yet to be lived. Let us hold them close, let us nurture them, and let us allow them to guide us on our journey. For in the end, it is not the destination that matters, but the journey itself – a journey of discovery, a journey of growth, and a journey of wonder.

we can see that expectations are the spark that sets our hearts ablaze with promise and possibility. They are the whispered secrets of a life yet to be lived, the hidden messages of a future yet to be written. They are the possibilities that tantalize, the maybes that mesmerize, and the what-ifs that haunt us.

And what better time to harness the power of expectations than in the month of January? As the calendar flips to a brand new year, we are filled with a sense of hope and renewal. The possibilities seem endless, and the promise of a fresh start is intoxicating.

January is the month when we set our resolutions, make our plans, and dream big. It's the month when we look to the future with optimism and anticipation, when we believe that anything is possible. And it's this sense of expectation that drives us forward, that motivates us to take action, and that inspires us to make our dreams a reality.

So, it's clear that January is not just any ordinary month. It's a month of new beginnings, of fresh starts, and of endless possibilities. It's a month when the world seems full of promise, and when our hearts are filled with hope and expectation.

And that's why it is clearly said that January is definitely the month of expectations. It's a time when we look to the future with anticipation, when we believe in ourselves and our abilities, and when we know that anything is possible.

As we close this chapter, we leave you with a sense of excitement and anticipation. What will the new year bring? What possibilities will unfold? What dreams will you make a reality?

The answer, of course, is up to you. But one thing is certain: January is the month of expectations, and it's the perfect time to start making your dreams come true.

Dear Self,

As I sit down to write to you, I am filled with a mix of emotions - nostalgia, regret, and a hint of wisdom. I want to talk to you about something that I've come to realize is a crucial part of life, but one that I've often overlooked. Expectations.

Expecting something from someone is like experiencing first love - oh so beautiful, yet so heartbroken. It's a feeling that fills your heart with hope and promise, only to leave you shattered and disappointed when reality sets in. And yet, we continue to expect, don't we?

As I look back, I realize that I was like a kid in January, full of expectations and anticipation. I expected the world to deliver on its promises. I expected people to behave in a certain way, and I expected life to unfold according to my plans. But life had other plans, and I was left feeling lost and disillusioned.

I am really sorry that I haven't mentioned it before, but rather than expectations, I should have focused more on acceptance. Life is all about working and accepting, not expecting and waiting. I wish I had understood this sooner.

I wish I had accepted that people will always be imperfect, that life will always be unpredictable, and that things will not always go according to plan. I wish I had accepted that it's okay to not have all the answers, that it's okay to make mistakes, and that it's okay to not be in control.

Most of all, I wish I had loved myself more. I wish I had been kinder to myself, more compassionate, and more understanding. I wish I had accepted myself for who I am, rather than trying to fit into someone else's expectations.

As I close this letter, I want to remind you that it's never too late to change. It's never too late to focus on acceptance rather than expectations. It's never too late to love yourself more, to be kinder to yourself, and to accept yourself for who you are.

So, dear self, let's make a promise to ourselves to focus on acceptance from now on. Let's promise to love ourselves more, to be kinder to ourselves, and to accept life for what it is – imperfect, unpredictable, and beautiful.

With love and acceptance,

Yourself

Chapter – 2

February: The Month of Reflections

"You can't connect the dots looking forward; you can only connect them looking backward. So you have to trust that the dots will somehow connect in your future."

- Steve Jobs

Rohan was a ticking time bomb, waiting to explode at any moment. His friends and family had grown accustomed to his short temper, but they never knew when he would blow up next.

It started with small things. A spilled cup of coffee, a misplaced phone charger, a delayed train. Rohan would get frustrated, his anger simmering just below the surface. He would mutter under his breath, his face reddening with rage.

One day, Rohan was driving to work when someone cut him off in traffic. He slammed on the brakes, his heart racing with anger. He honked the horn, yelling at the top of his lungs. The other driver, oblivious to Rohan's rage, simply drove away.

Rohan arrived at work, still fuming. His coworkers tried to calm him down, but he was having none of it. He snapped at them, his anger boiling over.

As the day went on, Rohan's anger only intensified. He got into a heated argument with a colleague, his voice rising to a shout. His manager had to intervene, sending Rohan home for the day.

Rohan stormed out of the office, his anger still simmering. He walked home, his feet pounding the pavement. He felt like he was going to explode.

When he arrived home, Rohan's wife, Priya, tried to calm him down. She asked him what was wrong, but Rohan just shook his head. He didn't know how to explain it. He just felt so angry all the time.

Priya tried to be patient, but she was getting worried. Rohan's anger was starting to affect their relationship. She didn't know how to deal with it.

As the days went by, Rohan's anger only got worse. He would lash out at Priya, at his friends, at strangers on the street. He felt like he was losing control.

One day, Rohan's anger boiled over in a way that would change everything. He was at the grocery store, shopping for dinner. A woman accidentally bumped into him, spilling his groceries all over the floor.

Rohan lost it. He yelled at the woman, his anger erupting like a volcano. The woman, startled, apologized and quickly left the store.

Rohan was left standing alone, his anger still simmering. But as he looked around at the mess he had made, he felt a pang of shame. He realized that his anger was not just affecting him, but those around him.

Rohan took a deep breath, trying to calm down. He knew he needed to get his anger under control. But as he looked at the mess on the floor, he wondered if it was too late.

Reality Check –

As Rohan sat in his apartment, lost in thought, he was aware of the tough times he had faced. But what weighed heavily on his mind was the realization that his struggles were not just his own. He knew that the patterns of behavior, the coping mechanisms, and the unresolved traumas that had been passed down to him from his parents would likely be passed down to his own children one day.

Rohan was aware that he was a product of his father's upbringing, and that his father was a reflection of his own grandfather's influence. He knew that he was destined to repeat the same patterns, to make the same mistakes, unless he made a conscious effort to break the cycle.

The thought of his children suffering the same generational trauma that he had endured was almost too much to bear. He knew that his father's inability to overcome his own demons had affected him deeply, and that he was at risk of passing on the same pain to his own kids. He thought about the absent parenting, the neglect, and the emotional scars that had been inflicted upon him, and he knew that he didn't want his children to suffer the same fate.

Rohan realized that he had a choice to make. He could continue down the same path, perpetuating the cycle of trauma and pain, or he could take a stand and break the chain. He could choose to be the one who ended the generational trauma, who created a new and healthier pattern for his children to follow.

As he looked to the future, Rohan knew that he had to make a change. Not for himself, not for his parents, but for his children's sake. He wanted to give them a better life, a life free from the burdens of the past. He wanted to be the parent that he had always needed, but never had.

With a newfound sense of determination, Rohan stood up, ready to face the challenges ahead. He knew that it wouldn't be easy, but he was willing to do whatever it took to break the cycle of trauma and create a brighter future for his children.

The Unseen Legacy of Generational Trauma

As we navigate the complexities of our own lives, it's easy to overlook the subtle yet profound impact of our family's history on our present. Generational trauma, a phenomenon where the emotional and psychological wounds of our ancestors are passed down through generations, can have a profound effect on our well-being, relationships, and overall quality of life.

So, how does generational trauma work? When our ancestors experience traumatic events, such as war, abuse, or loss, their bodies respond by releasing stress hormones like cortisol and adrenaline. This stress response can become stuck, leading to changes in their brain chemistry, behavior, and even gene expression. These changes can then be passed down to their children and grandchildren through various mechanisms, including epigenetics, social learning, and family dynamics.

As a result, individuals may experience a range of symptoms, including anxiety, depression, addiction, and relationship problems, without realizing that these issues may be linked to their family's past. Generational trauma can also manifest in more subtle ways, such as self-sabotaging patterns, people-pleasing, or an intense need for control.

The consequences of generational trauma can be far-reaching, affecting not only individuals but also entire families and communities. It can lead to cycles of violence, abuse, and addiction, as well as perpetuate social and economic inequalities.

So, what can we do to break free from the cycle of generational trauma? The first step is to acknowledge and accept our family's history, rather than trying to suppress or deny it. This involves developing a curiosity about our ancestors' experiences and how they may have shaped our own lives.

As we reflect on our family's past, we may begin to notice patterns and themes that have been passed down through generations. We may realize that our own struggles and strengths are connected to the struggles and strengths of our ancestors. This awareness can be both empowering and liberating, allowing us to make conscious choices about the kind of life we want to lead.

A Month of Reflection

As we enter the month of February, a time of reflection and introspection, let us take a moment to consider the unseen legacy of generational trauma. Let us acknowledge the ways in which our family's past may be shaping our present, and take the first steps towards breaking free from the cycle of trauma.

By doing so, we can begin to heal and transform our lives, creating a brighter future for ourselves and our loved ones. We can learn to recognize the patterns and themes that have been passed down through generations and make conscious choices about the kind of life we want to lead.

In this month of reflection, let us take the time to explore our family's history, to listen to the stories of our ancestors, and to acknowledge the ways in which their experiences may be shaping our own. By doing so, we can begin to break free from the cycle of generational trauma and create a more compassionate, resilient, and fulfilling life.

Dear Little One,

As I sit down to write this letter to you, I'm filled with a mix of emotions - love, hope, and a hint of sadness. I'm not sure when you'll read this, but I want you to know that I'm writing this for you, for us, and for the life we're going to build together.

I want to be honest with you, kiddo. I've been through some tough times in my life. There have been moments when I felt like giving up, when the darkness seemed to consume me, and when I thought I couldn't take it anymore. I've struggled with depression for 9 long years, and anxiety has been my constant companion. There have been times when I felt like I was drowning, and I didn't know how to keep my head above water.

But here's the thing, little one. I'm still here. I'm still fighting. And I'm fighting not just for myself, but for you. I want you to know that I'm doing everything in my power to break the cycle of trauma and pain that has been passed down through our family. I don't want you to go through what I went through. I don't want you to feel the same pain, the same fear, and the same doubt that I felt.

I know that I may not have had the most ideal childhood, and I may not have had the happiest of experiences. But I want you to know that I'm committed to creating a different life for you. I want you to grow up in a home filled with love, laughter, and joy. I want you to feel safe, supported, and encouraged to be your amazing self.

I know that I'm not perfect, and I'll make mistakes along the way. But I promise you that I'll do my best to be the parent you deserve. I'll be patient, kind, and understanding. I'll listen to you, I'll validate your feelings, and I'll be there for you whenever you need me.

I want you to know that life is beautiful, kiddo. It's messy, it's complicated, and it's unpredictable, but it's also full of wonder, magic, and joy. I want you to experience all the beauty that life has to offer, and I want to be there to guide you every step of the way.

I may not have had the happiest of childhoods, but I'm determined to create a happy, healthy, and loving home for you. I'll do everything in my power to make sure that you don't inherit my trauma, my pain, and my fears. Instead, I'll pass on my love, my hope, and my resilience.

I love you more than words can express, little one. You're the light of my life, and I'm so grateful to be your parent. I promise to do my best to be the parent you deserve, and to create a life that's filled with love, laughter, and joy.

With all my love,

Mom/Dad

Chapter – 3

March: A Month of Hope

"Hope is being able to see that there is light despite all the darkness"

- Desmond Tutu

March 2025 was a month that would be etched in the memories of every Indian cricket fan forever. It was a month of transition, a month of triumph, and a month of hope.

For 12 long years, the Indian cricket team had struggled to reclaim their spot at the top of the cricketing world. They had faced setbacks, disappointments, and heartbreaks, but they had never given up hope. And finally, their perseverance had paid off.

As the Indian team, led by captain Rohit Sharma, lifted the ICC ODI Champions Trophy aloft, the nation erupted in joy. Every Indian, from the streets of Mumbai to the villages of Kerala, celebrated the team's victory with pride and passion.

But this victory was not just about the team; it was about every Indian who had supported them through thick and thin. It was about the hopes and dreams of a nation, which had been kept alive by the team's unwavering determination.

As the team's journey to success unfolded, every Indian could connect with their struggles and triumphs. They remembered the heartbreaking losses, the thrilling victories, and the moments of pure magic that had defined the team's journey.

And then, there was the World Cup victory in 2024, which had marked a turning point for the team. Who could forget the nail-biting final match against Australia, where Virat Kohli's brilliant innings and KL Rahul's valuable contribution had helped India chase down a target of 320 runs in 50 overs?

As the team celebrated their Champions Trophy victory, every Indian knew that this was not just a triumph of cricket; it was a triumph of hope. It was a reminder that no matter how tough the journey may seem, hope can be the catalyst that drives us towards our dreams.

And so, as the Indian team basked in the glory of their victory, every Indian knew that they had been a part of something special. They had been a part of a journey that had inspired a nation, a journey that had kept hope alive, and a journey that would continue to inspire generations to come.

Carry Your Hope Wherever You Go

Hope is the beacon that illuminates our path, guiding us through life's challenges and uncertainties. It's the spark that ignites our passions, fuels our dreams, and gives us the courage to persevere.

After kindness, hope is the most precious gift we can give ourselves and others. It's the bridge that connects our past, present, and future, reminding us that every experience, no matter how difficult, is an opportunity for growth and learning.

So, bear your hope with you, wherever you go. Don't let anyone or anything extinguish its flame. Nurture it, cherish it, and let it guide you through life's journey.

It doesn't matter what shade your hope comes in – bright and bold, or soft and subtle. What matters is that it brings you comfort, peace, and happiness.

Remember, today was once a yesterday you prayed for. And if today isn't the day you've been waiting for, have hope that tomorrow will bring new opportunities, new experiences, and new reasons to celebrate.

As we say ladies and gentlemen, "Umeed pe toh duniya kayam hai" – The world survives on hope.

But remember, my love, life is unpredictable. No matter how carefully you plan, how hard you work, or how much you wish, there will always come a drop in your life that will take you to your lowest.

It may be a failure, a loss, a heartbreak, or a setback. But here's the thing: life doesn't end there. You don't have to let that one drop define your entire journey.

So, hope for what you wish for, always and forever. Hope for a brighter tomorrow, a better today, and a chance to start anew.

Hope is the light that shines in the darkness, guiding you through the toughest of times. It's the voice that whispers "you can" when everyone else says "you can't."

So, hold on to hope, dear ones. Let it be your guiding light, your safe haven, and your reason to keep moving forward. For with hope, anything is possible, and every day is a new chance to create a brighter, more beautiful tomorrow.

Dear You,

In the midst of life's chaos, I want you to remember that you are a beacon of hope. Today may seem overwhelming, but I urge you to tap into the resilience that lies within you.

Life is a masterful teacher, weaving lessons into every experience. Its unpredictability can be harsh, but it's also a catalyst for growth. You are a student of life, and every challenge is an opportunity to learn and rise.

I want you to know that you're doing better than you think. Your strength is not measured by your struggles, but by your ability to face them head-on. You are a warrior, armed with courage and determination.

Don't let hope flicker out. You are capable of achieving greatness, of overcoming obstacles, and of emerging stronger. Your success is not defined by today's struggles, but by the fact that you've made it through each day with unwavering spirit.

You are a shining example of resilience, a testament to the human spirit's ability to persevere. Keep moving forward, even when the steps feel small. Every journey begins with a single step, and every great achievement is born from the courage to keep going.

One day, you'll look back on your struggles and smile, knowing that you emerged victorious. You'll be proud of yourself, and you'll be ready to face whatever tomorrow brings.

Live your life to the fullest, my friend. You are a masterpiece in progress, and every experience is a brushstroke on the canvas of your story. You got this!

With love and unwavering support,
A Kind Heart

Chapter – 4

The April Awakening

"The love of Krishna is the ultimate reality, the source of all joy, and the destination of all spiritual seeking."

- Radhanath Swami

The Eternal Embrace of Lord Krishna: A Journey of Inner Awakening

As we embark on this sacred journey, let us first immerse ourselves in the divine presence of Lord Krishna. Allow your heart to be enveloped by his loving energy, and permit your soul to be stirred by his eternal wisdom.

Imagine yourself standing on the sun-kissed banks of the Yamuna River, surrounded by the lush greenery of the Indian countryside. The air is filled with the sweet fragrance of blooming flowers, and the soft rustling of leaves carried by the gentle breeze.

As you close your eyes, feel the warmth of Lord Krishna's presence enveloping you. His eyes, like the infinite expanse of the cosmos, shine bright with compassion and knowledge. They sparkle with a mischievous glint, hinting at the divine secrets hidden within.

His gaze is a gentle breeze that soothes your soul, calming the turbulent waters of your mind. His face, a masterpiece of divine craftsmanship, radiates a warm, golden light. It is a canvas of serenity, reflecting the depths of his wisdom and the heights of his love.

As you breathe in deeply, feel the essence of Lord Krishna's being merge with yours. His smile, a gentle whisper of encouragement, dispels the darkest of doubts and ignites the flame of hope within your heart.

His body, a temple of strength and agility, is a testament to his divine heritage. His dark, velvety skin glistens with an ethereal sheen, as if infused with the essence of the stars.

As you stand before him, feel the boundaries of reality expand, and the limits of time and space dissolve. You are in the presence of the ultimate truth, the source of all creation, and the wellspring of infinite wisdom.

The Awakening of Reality: A Journey of Healing and Transformation

As the battle-scarred warriors of the Pandava and Kaurava armies faced off on the dusty plains of Kurukshetra, Arjuna, the mighty warrior, stood frozen in despair. His eyes, once bright with courage and conviction, now dimly gazed upon the familiar faces of his kin, his friends, and his former teachers.

The weight of his dilemma crushed him, like the mighty mountains that towered above the battlefield. His heart, once a fortress of strength and valor, now lay shattered, like the fragile petals of a flower trampled beneath the feet of a raging elephant.

As he gazed upon the sea of faces before him, Arjuna's mind recoiled in horror. How could he raise his arms against those he loved and respected? How could he bring himself to fight against his own kin, his own guru, and his own friends?

The turmoil within him reached a boiling point, and Arjuna's body trembled with the intensity of his emotions. His eyes, brimming with tears, pleaded for guidance, for solace, and for a way out of the abyss that seemed to swallow him whole.

It was then that Lord Krishna, the charioteer of Arjuna, reached out with a gentle hand, and touched the warrior's trembling heart.

"Arjuna, my beloved friend and disciple," Krishna began, his voice a soothing balm to the warrior's troubled mind, "why do you falter? Why do you hesitate to fulfill your duty as a warrior?"

Arjuna, his voice cracking with emotion, poured out his heart to Krishna. "How can I fight against my own kin, my own guru, and my own friends? How can I bring myself to raise my arms against those I love and respect?"

Krishna's gaze, a gentle breeze that soothed Arjuna's soul, calmed the turbulent waters of his mind. "Arjuna, the reality you seek is not something to be found outside; it lies within. The ultimate truth is not a distant horizon, but the very essence of your being."

As Krishna's words poured like a soothing balm into Arjuna's troubled mind, the warrior's eyes began to see beyond the veil of confusion. His heart, once heavy with doubt, now swelled with the courage of conviction.

"Remember, Arjuna," Krishna continued, "the world is a mere reflection of the divine. Every experience, every challenge, and every triumph is an opportunity to awaken to the ultimate reality."

As Arjuna listened to Krishna's words, his perception shifted. He saw the world anew, bathed in the golden light of Krishna's wisdom. His doubts dissipated, replaced by an unwavering faith in the divine plan.

In that moment, Arjuna's heart, once shattered by the weight of his dilemma, was healed by the gentle touch of Krishna's love. The warrior's eyes, once dimly gazing upon the battlefield, now shone bright with courage and conviction.

As we reflect on this sacred conversation, we are reminded that our devotion to Lord Krishna is, in itself, the awakening of reality. By surrendering to his divine presence, we invite the ultimate truth to reside within us.

May our hearts, like Arjuna's, be healed by the gentle touch of Krishna's love, and may our devotion to Lord Krishna guide us on the path of self-discovery and growth.

As the Bhagavad Gita so eloquently states:

"Man mana bhava mad bhakto, mad yaji mam namaskuru; Mam evaisyasi yuktvaivam, atmanam mat parayanah."

"Fix your mind on me, be devoted to me, worship me, and offer obeisance to me. Thus, with your mind fixed on me, you will come to me alone."

(Bhagavad Gita, Chapter 9, Verse 34)

May we, like Arjuna, fix our minds on Lord Krishna, and may our hearts be forever transformed by the eternal embrace of his love.

Connecting with the Divine: A Journey into the Heart of Lord Krishna

As we immerse ourselves in the divine presence of Lord Krishna, let us embark on a journey into the very heart of the universe. Allow your mind to settle, like a calm lake on a windless day, reflecting the infinite beauty of the divine.

Feel the warmth of Krishna's presence enveloping you, soothing your worries, and calming your doubts. With each breath, allow your heart to open, like a lotus flower blooming in the radiant light of the sun.

As you inhale, repeat the sacred mantra:

"Krishnaye Vasudevaye Haraye Paramatmane

Pranata-Klesha-Nashaye Govindaye Namo Namah"

(Salutations to Lord Krishna, the son of Vasudeva, the remover of all suffering, the supreme self, and the destroyer of all afflictions.")

Feel the vibrations of this ancient prayer resonating deep within your soul, awakening the dormant seeds of devotion and love.

As you exhale, feel the tension, anxiety, and fear leaving your body, like autumn leaves drifting gently to the ground. Allow yourself to settle into a state of inner peace, where the boundaries of reality expand, and the limits of time and space dissolve.

In this sacred space, imagine Lord Krishna standing before you, his eyes shining with compassion and love. Feel his gentle touch on your heart, soothing your deepest wounds, and awakening your highest potential.

As you bask in the radiance of Krishna's presence, remember that you are not separate from the divine. You are an integral part of the universe, a droplet of the infinite ocean of love and consciousness.

In this state of unity and connection, may you experience the eternal embrace of Lord Krishna's love, guiding you on the path of self-discovery and growth. May your heart be filled with devotion, your mind be illuminated with wisdom, and your soul be forever transformed by the divine presence of Lord Krishna.

Dear Arjuna (My beloved Heart),

As you stand on the battlefield of life, I, Krishna (Your Consciousness), stand beside you, guiding and directing you toward your highest potential. The winds of destiny whisper secrets in my ear, and I shall share them with you, my beloved heart.

Remember, you are a warrior, not merely a survivor. Your heart beats with the rhythm of dharma, and you have consistently chosen the path of righteousness, even in the face of adversity. Your courage is a beacon of light, illuminating the darkness, and inspiring others to follow in your footsteps.

As I shared with you in the Bhagavad Gita:

"Karmanye vadhikaraste, Ma Phaleshu Kadachana"

"You have the right to perform your prescribed duties, but never to the fruits of your actions."

(Bhagavad Gita, Chapter 2, Verse 47)

Do not let doubts and fears assail your mind. I am always with you, guiding and protecting you at every step. My presence is the calm in every storm, the safe haven where you can anchor your soul. Have faith in my plan, and trust that everything will unfold in your favor.

As you navigate the complexities of life, remember that you are not alone. I am the charioteer of your soul, steering you toward the ultimate truth. My whispers are the gentle breeze that soothes your heart, and my guidance is the shining light that illuminates your path.

In moments of confusion and despair, repeat the eternal promise:

कृष्ण·सदा·सहायते

(I, Krishna, am always ready to help)

As I shared with you in the Mahabharata:

"Yada yada hi dharmasya, glanirbhavati bharata"

"Whenever dharma declines, O Bharata, and adharma rises, I manifest myself."

(Mahabharata, Bhagavad Gita, Chapter 4, Verse 7)

Feel my presence enveloping you, soothing your worries, and calming your doubts. I am the ocean of love and consciousness, and you are a droplet of my divine essence.

Never lose hope, for I am always with you, guiding and directing you toward your highest potential. You are a spark of my divine light, and I shall fan the flames of your heart, until you shine brighter than the brightest star.

May my words be etched in your heart, and may you forever be connected to my divine presence.

As I shared with you in the Bhagavad Gita:

"Man mana bhava mad bhakto, mad yaji mam namaskuru"

"Fix your mind on me, be devoted to me, worship me, and offer obeisance to me."

(Bhagavad Gita, Chapter 9, Verse 34)

With love

Krishna

Your forever charioteer ☺

Chapter – 5

May: The Month of Letting Go

"Some people believe holding on and hanging in there are signs of great strength. However, there are times when it takes much more strength to know when to let go and then do it."

- Ann Landers

The Cycle of letting Go

Sakshi's eyes sparkled as she gazed at Rudra, her heart overflowing with love and adoration. For what felt like an eternity, she had been waiting for him to commit, to take their relationship to the next level. But Rudra, with his chiseled features and captivating smile, seemed perpetually stuck in neutral.

At 26, Sakshi was ready to settle down, to build a life with the man she loved. But Rudra, 29 and charming, was haunted by the ghosts of his past. His first love, a relationship that began when he was just 16, had left an indelible mark on his heart. Despite the passage of time and a string of subsequent relationships, Rudra couldn't shake off the memories of his ex.

As Sakshi waited patiently for Rudra to come around, she began to realize that she was stuck, too. She had created a mental script of their future together, a fairy tale romance that seemed increasingly unlikely. Life, Sakshi was learning, doesn't always follow our scripts.

The cycle of their emotions was a vicious one: Rudra was stuck on his ex, and Sakshi was stuck on Rudra. If they wanted to be happy, they both needed to let go. Rudra must release his emotions and feelings for his ex, acknowledging that what's gone will never come back. Sakshi must let go of her attachment to Rudra and the future she envisioned with him.

One day, Sakshi stumbled upon a quote that resonated deeply with her: "Letting go doesn't mean that you don't care about someone anymore. It's just realizing that the only person you really have control over is yourself." She realized that she couldn't change Rudra or his feelings, but she could change herself. She could choose to let go.

With a newfound sense of determination, Sakshi began to release her attachment to Rudra. She started focusing on herself, her passions, and her goals. She practiced yoga, meditation, and journaling, slowly unraveling the threads of her emotional baggage.

Rudra, too, began to sense the shift in Sakshi's energy. He saw the change in her, the way she carried herself with a newfound confidence and self-awareness. And though it scared him, he knew he had to confront his own demons. He started therapy, working through his unresolved emotions and learning to let go of his past.

As Sakshi and Rudra navigated their respective journeys, they began to realize that letting go wasn't about erasing the past or forgetting the memories.

It was about acknowledging the pain, releasing the emotional baggage, and embracing the present with an open heart.

Their story serves as a poignant reminder that letting go is essential for growth, for moving forward. By releasing our attachment to people, emotions, and experiences, we create space for new relationships, new experiences, and new versions of ourselves.

As Sakshi and Rudra's paths continued to unfold, they knew that they would always carry a piece of each other with them. But they also knew that they had to let go, to release the cycle of emotions that had held them back for so long. In doing so, they discovered that the true beauty of letting go lies not in the release itself, but in the freedom, the growth, and the transformation that follows.

The Art of letting go: Jaane Do!

"Listen up, friend! Take a deep breath, and let's get real for a moment. You know what's holding you back? It's the emotional baggage you've been carrying around for far too long. It's the memories, the pain, the people who no longer serve you.

Newsflash: not everyone is meant to stay in your life! Some people are only meant to be there for a reason, a season, or a lifetime. And when their time is up, it's okay to let them go! It's okay to acknowledge the pain, the lessons, and the growth, and then release it all.

You deserve peace, freedom, and liberation! And the only way to get that is to let go of what's holding you back. It's not about erasing the past or forgetting memories; it's about releasing the emotional weight that's keeping you stuck.

Think about it: every experience, every relationship, and every memory has shaped you into the person you are today. But that doesn't mean you need to carry it all with you. You can acknowledge the lessons, the love, and the laughter, and then let it go.

And here's the thing: letting go is a sign of STRENGTH, not weakness! It takes courage to release what's familiar, even if it's no longer serving you. It takes courage to walk away from the comfort zone, to step into the unknown, and to trust that you'll find your way.

And remember, just because someone is good, it doesn't mean they're right for you. You deserve someone who is not only good but also right for you. Someone who lifts you up, supports you, and loves you for who you are.

So, I want you to take a deep breath, stand up straight, and declare to the universe: "I'm letting go! I'm releasing the past, the pain, and the people who no longer serve me. I'm embracing the present with an open heart, and I'm ready to soar!"

Repeat it with me: "I'm letting go! I'm releasing the past, the pain, and the people who no longer serve me. I'm embracing the present with an open heart, and I'm ready to soar!"

Feel the weight lifting off your shoulders? Feel the freedom, the peace, and the liberation? That's what letting go can do for you.

You got this, friend! You have the strength, the courage, and the resilience to let go of what's holding you back. So, go ahead, take the leap, and watch yourself soar!"

Why we Struggle to Let Go:

1. We think holding on is a sign of strength: We often believe that holding on to a relationship, a memory, or a past experience is a sign of strength and loyalty. However, this couldn't be further from the truth. Holding on to something that's no longer serving us can be a sign of fear, insecurity, and a lack of self-awareness.

2. We're so hurt that we don't have the capacity to move on: Trauma, heartbreak, and pain can be overwhelming, making it difficult for us to process our emotions and move forward. We might feel stuck in a cycle of hurt and anger, unable to envision a future without the pain.

3. We're stuck on the question "Why me?" When we're hurt or wronged, it's natural to wonder why it happened to us. However, getting stuck on this question can prevent us from moving forward. We might become obsessed with finding answers, rehashing the past, and reliving the pain.

4. We're waiting for closure: Closure is a myth. It's a concept we've created to help us cope with the uncertainty of life. However, waiting for closure can keep us stuck in the past, preventing us from embracing the present and future.

5. We're habitual of hurting ourselves: Sometimes, we're so accustomed to pain and suffering that we don't know how to live without it. We might sabotage our relationships, engage in self-destructive behaviors, or hold on to toxic emotions because they're familiar.

How to let go:

1. We think holding on is a sign of strength:

- "It's time to redefine strength. Letting go doesn't mean you're weak; it means you're brave enough to release the weights that hold you back. Allow yourself to be vulnerable, to feel the emotions, and to let go of the need to control. Remember, strength lies not in holding on, but in embracing the unknown."

2. We're so hurt that we don't have the capacity to move on:

- "Your heart is broken, but it's not shattered. It's still beating, still pumping life into your veins. Allow yourself to feel the pain, but don't let it define you. You are more than your hurt. You are strong, resilient, and capable of healing. Take small steps towards moving forward, and remember that every step forward is a victory."

3. We're stuck on the question "Why me?"

- "The question 'Why me?' is a labyrinth with no exit. It's a cycle of self-doubt and blame. But what if you asked yourself a different question? What if you asked, 'What can I learn from this experience?' or 'How can I grow from this pain?' Shift your perspective, and you'll find that the answers you seek are within you all along."

4. We're waiting for closure:

- "Closure is a myth, a mirage on the horizon of our minds. But what if you didn't need closure to move forward? What if you could create your own closure by acknowledging the experience, processing your emotions, and choosing to let go? You have the power to create your own closure, to write your own ending to the story. So, take a deep breath, and start writing."

5. We're habitual of hurting ourselves:

- "You are not a slave to your pain. You are not a prisoner of your past. You are a warrior, a survivor, a thriver. It's time to break free from the cycle of self-destructive behaviors and to learn to love yourself instead. Remember, you are worthy of love, care, and compassion – not just from others, but from yourself as well."

Hence:

- "Acknowledge your emotions, and give yourself permission to feel. It's okay to not be okay, and it's okay to take your time."

   - "Practice self-compassion, and treat yourself with kindness, understanding, and patience. You are doing the best you can and that's enough."

   - "Reframe your perspective, and challenge negative thoughts. You have the power to choose how you see the world, so choose to see it with hope, optimism, and joy."

   - "Create distance, and establish physical and emotional boundaries. You deserve to be safe, respected, and loved."

   - "Focus on the present, and engage in activities that bring you joy. Mindfulness is a powerful tool for healing, growth, and transformation."

- "Seek support, and surround yourself with people who uplift, encourage, and support you. You don't have to do it alone."

- "Practice forgiveness, and remember that forgiveness doesn't mean forgetting or condoning. Forgiveness means releasing the emotional weight that's holding you back."

- "Create new routines, and try new activities. You are capable of growth, change, and transformation."

- "Practice gratitude, and focus on the things you're thankful for. Gratitude is a powerful tool for shifting your perspective and finding joy in the present moment."

- "Celebrate your growth, and acknowledge your progress. You are doing the best you can, and that's something to be proud of."

Dear Future Self,

I'm writing to you today from the past, with tears of joy and gratitude in my eyes. As I sit down to pen this letter, I'm filled with a sense of pride and accomplishment, knowing that I've worked tirelessly to get you to where you are today.

If today you're able to breathe easily, feeling the warmth of the sun on your skin and the gentle rustle of the wind in your hair, it's because I let go of the suffocating grip of anxiety and fear. I released the weight of worry, allowing you to live life to the fullest, unencumbered by the burdens of yesterday.

If today you're living a life you once imagined, with dreams transformed into reality, it's because I dared to believe in myself, even when the world around me seemed uncertain. I took the leap of faith, and you're now reaping the rewards of that courage.

If today your scars don't hurt you anymore, it's because I faced them head-on, allowing the wounds to heal, and the pain to subside. I learned to love and accept myself, flaws and all, and you're now basking in the warmth of self-love and self-acceptance.

If today you have this beautiful, loving family that you built on your own, it's because I took the time to nurture relationships, to invest in people, and to cultivate love. I weeded out the toxic connections, making space for the loving, supportive ones that now surround you.

If today you're not scared of anything, it's because I faced my fears, one by one, and emerged victorious. I learned to trust myself, to trust the universe, and to trust that everything will work out for your highest good.

If today you know that at the end, things will get alright, it's because I practiced faith, patience, and perseverance. I learned to trust in the natural order of life, to have faith in the unknown, and to know that every challenge is an opportunity for growth.

If today you have nothing but kindness and love in your heart, it's because I made a conscious choice to let go of negativity, to release resentment, and to cultivate compassion.

I chose to see the good in everyone, to love unconditionally, and to spread joy wherever you go.

All of this, dear Future Self, is a testament to the power of letting go. I let go of the past, of fear, of anxiety, of negativity, and of doubt. I let go of everything that held me back, and in doing so, I created space for you to thrive.

I'm proud of you, dear Future Self. I'm proud of the person you've become, of the life you've built, and of the love you share with the world. Keep shining, keep loving, and keep letting go.

With love and gratitude,

Your Past Self

Chapter – 6

June: The Month of Authenticity

"To be free is not merely to cast off one's chains, but to live in a way that respects and enhances the freedom of others."

- Nelson Mandela

The Masked Workplace

Rhea had always been an exemplary employee. She worked tirelessly, delivered high-quality results, and was kind to everyone in the office. Her colleagues admired her, and her boss praised her.

However, beneath the surface, Rhea was suffocating. She was too genuine, too authentic, and too transparent in a workplace where masks and facades reigned supreme.

Her colleagues would often compliment her on her work, only to stab her in the back when opportunities arose. Her boss would praise her publicly, but privately, would manipulate her into taking on more workload without recognition or reward.

Rhea tried to navigate this treacherous landscape, but it was exhausting. She felt like she was losing herself in the process, forced to wear different masks to appease different people.

But what bothered her most was the feeling of being stuck. She felt like she was barely growing mentally and emotionally, like her creativity and potential were being stifled by the limited opportunities and toxic environment.

"I'm not learning anymore," Rhea would tell herself. "I'm not growing. I'm just existing."

One day, after three years of dedicated service, Rhea reached her breaking point. She realized that she couldn't continue to sacrifice her mental and emotional well-being for a job that didn't value her authenticity.

With a heavy heart, Rhea submitted her resignation. As she packed her belongings and said goodbye to her colleagues, she felt a sense of relief wash over her.

"You're too good for this place," a colleague whispered, as Rhea hugged her goodbye.

Rhea smiled, knowing that she was leaving behind a workplace that valued masks over authenticity. She was ready to start anew, to find a place where her genuineness was cherished, not suffocated.

As she walked out of the office building, Rhea felt the warm sun on her face, and a sense of freedom in her heart. She knew that she would find a workplace where she could be herself, without apology or pretension.

A place where she could grow, learn, and thrive.

The masked workplace was behind her, and a brighter, more authentic future lay ahead.

The Highest form of Vibrational Frequency: Authenticity

"Today, I want to ignite a fire within you. A fire that burns brightly with the flames of authenticity. Being your truest self is not just a choice, it's a superpower. It's the highest expression of yourself, and it's the key to unlocking your true potential.

We live in a world where masks are worn like armor, and conformity is often prioritized over individuality. But I want you to know that you don't have to be a slave to societal expectations. You don't have to wear a mask to hide your true self.

Psychologically, we know that living a life of inauthenticity can lead to feelings of disorientation, confusion, and anxiety. It's like living in a constant state of disconnection from your true nature. But what if I told you that there's a way to break free from this cycle?

Authenticity is not just a moral virtue; it's a psychological imperative. When you're true to yourself, you're more grounded, more confident, and more resilient. You're better able to navigate life's challenges and to build meaningful relationships.

But you know what, whenever we are disconnected from our true forms, we are advised to go to nature or be connected to nature. You know why? Because there, you understand your roots; it connects you with your roots. Secondly, when you sit with yourself, you solve yourself like you solve a puzzle.

Many people who are not their truest form or who are living in a different world, they actually don't sit with themselves. That's why they don't know who they are, and this is one of the reasons they have failed careers, failed relationships.

But here's the thing: you have the power to change that. You have the power to sit with yourself, to listen to your inner voice, and to uncover your truest form.

I want to share something personal with you. Whenever I'm in a state of confusion or feeling low, I isolate myself from the world. I sleep, I eat, and then I sit with myself. I talk to myself, asking, 'What energy am I unable to understand? What is my body and mind rejecting?'

And you know what? In those moments of solitude, I discover new aspects of myself. I gain clarity, I find my strength, and I emerge stronger, wiser, and more authentic.

So, I want to leave you with a challenge today. I want to challenge you to do the same. When you're feeling lost, take a step back, and reconnect with nature. Sit with yourself, and ask those hard questions. Listen to your inner voice, and trust your intuition.

Remember, authenticity is a journey, not a destination. It takes courage, vulnerability, and self-awareness. But I promise you, my friend, it's worth it.

So, go out there and be your truest self. Be authentic, be brave, and be unapologetically you. You are a unique and precious gem, and the world needs your authenticity.

Don't let anyone dull your sparkle. Don't let anyone silence your voice. You are a force to be reckoned with, and your authenticity is the key to unlocking your true potential.

Go out there and shine!

Dear Rhea,

I want you to know that you're not alone in feeling suffocated by the weight of expectations, masks, and toxic environments. Many of us have been in your shoes, struggling to breathe, to think, and to be ourselves.

But here's the thing: you are brave. You are courageous. You are strong. And you are worthy of so much more. Your worth is not defined by your job, your relationships, or your external circumstances. Your worth is defined by your inherent value as a human being.

You are unique, talented, and gifted in ways that no one else is. And when you're able to tap into that uniqueness, that's when the magic happens. But I know it's not easy. I know it's hard to break free from the shackles of expectation and conformity.

It's hard to be different, to stand out, to be authentic. But here's the thing: authenticity is not just a virtue, it's a superpower. When you're able to be yourself, without apology or pretension, that's when you're able to tap into your deepest potential.

So, I want to leave you with a challenge today. I want to challenge you to be brave, to be courageous, and to be authentic. I want to challenge you to take off the masks, to shed the expectations, and to be yourself, fully and unapologetically.

It won't be easy. There will be people who don't understand, who don't support you, and who may even try to bring you down. But I want you to remember that their opinions, their judgments, and their expectations are not your responsibility.

Your responsibility is to yourself. Your responsibility is to be true to yourself, to honor your values, and to live your life with purpose and intention.

So, go out there and be you. Be the best version of yourself, without apology or pretension. Be authentic, be brave, and be unapologetically you.

And remember, my friend, you are not alone. There are people out there who will support you, who will encourage you, and who will celebrate your uniqueness.

You got this. You are strong, you are capable, and you are worthy of living an authentic, meaningful, and fulfilling life.

Go out there and crush it!

With all love,

Your true self ☺

Chapter – 7

July: The Month of Kindness

"Treat others the way you want to be treated. It's a simple philosophy, but it's one that can make a huge difference in the lives of those around you."

- Joe Girard

Dhruv's life had been a testament to the power of kindness. As a renowned clinical psychologist, he had helped countless individuals navigate the complexities of their minds. But his journey to this point had not been easy.

Dhruv's father had passed away when he was just in the 9th grade. The loss had left him reeling, and he became withdrawn and quiet. It wasn't until he met Kavya while preparing for his medical exams that he finally found a friend.

Kavya was a kind and compassionate soul, always ready to lend a listening ear or a helping hand. Dhruv was drawn to her warmth and empathy, and soon found himself opening up to her in ways he never thought possible.

One day, Dhruv asked Kavya, "How do you manage to be so kind to everyone, even when they're unkind to you?"

Kavya's response was profound. "My mother taught me that life and people will often be unfair to you, but that doesn't define who you are. You have to be kind because you never know what someone is going through."

Kavya shared a story about a friend she had in Bangalore who had struggled with depression. The friend had made some poor choices while struggling with her mental health, and people had judged her harshly. When she needed help, there was no one to turn to. The lack of kindness and understanding had ultimately led to a devastating outcome – the friend had attempted suicide.

Kavya's eyes welled up with tears as she spoke. "It was like she was murdered by the unkindness of those around her. That's why I always try to be kind to everyone, because I never know what they're going through."

Dhruv was deeply moved by Kavya's words. From that day on, he made a conscious effort to be kind to everyone he met. He listened to their stories, offered words of encouragement, and helped in any way he could.

As Dhruv's kindness grew, so did his reputation as a compassionate and empathetic psychologist. People came from all over to seek his counsel, and he helped them navigate the darkest corners of their minds.

Years later, Dhruv looked back on his journey and realized that Kavya's words had been the catalyst for his transformation. He had learned that kindness was not just a virtue, but a necessity – a necessity that could change lives and save souls.

As Dhruv sat in his office, surrounded by the stories of those he had helped, he felt a sense of pride and purpose. He knew that he had made a difference in the world, one act of kindness at a time.

And as he looked out the window, he saw Kavya's smiling face in his mind's eye, reminding him of the power of kindness to transform lives.

The story of Dhruv and Kavya serves as a poignant reminder that kindness is not just a feeling, but a choice. It's a choice to see the humanity in others, to listen to their stories, and to offer a helping hand. And it's a choice that can change the world, one act at a time.

"Choose Kindness: A Journey to Change The World, One Act at a Time"

Today I want to talk to you about something that has the power to transform lives, to heal wounds, and to bring people together. Something that is often overlooked, but never overvalued. That something is kindness.

Kindness is more than just a feeling or an action. It's a way of being. It's a choice to see the humanity in others, to listen to their stories, and to offer a helping hand. It's a choice to be present, to be patient, and to be understanding.

When someone allows you to know their pain, it's a sacred trust. It's a privilege to be let into their inner world, to see their vulnerability, and to hear their story. In that moment, take off your shoes and sit. Show them that you're willing to listen, to learn, and to be present.

This is a holy place, where vulnerability meets compassion. Be humble, be gentle, and be kind. Remember that everyone has a story, everyone has a struggle, and everyone has a pain. And when they share that with you, it's a gift.

So, what can you do with this gift? You can offer kindness. You can offer empathy. You can offer compassion. You can offer a listening ear, a comforting word, and a helping hand.

Teach kindness to anyone who will listen. Teach it to your children, your friends, your family, and your community. Teach it to yourself. Because kindness is the greatest virtue, the most pure form of love.

Kindness is an art. It's a way of living, a way of being. It's a choice to see the good in people, to see the beauty in the world, and to see the potential in every situation.

Show kindness in your voice, in your actions, and in your heart. You never know what people are going through. You never know what struggles they're facing, what pains they're hiding, or what fears they're carrying.

So, be kind. Be gentle. Be compassionate. Be understanding. Be patient. Be present.

Yes, people can be mean. They can be rude. They can be hurtful. But you be your true form. Wear kindness like a badge of honor. Wear it like a crown.

Because the antidote to rudeness is kindness. The antidote to hate is love. The antidote to fear is compassion.

So, let's make a choice today. Let's choose kindness. Let's choose compassion. Let's choose love.

Let's create a world where kindness is the norm, where empathy is the standard, and where compassion is the guiding principle.

Let's make kindness mesmerizing, comfortable, and inspiring. Let's make it contagious, infectious, and irresistible.

Let's spread kindness like wildfire, like a revolution, like a movement.

Let's start today. Let's start now. Let's start with ourselves.

Let's be kind. Let's be compassionate. Let's be love.

Because when we are kind, we are not just changing the world, we are changing ourselves. We are becoming the best version of ourselves, the kindest, most compassionate, and most loving version of ourselves.

So, let's do it. Let's choose kindness. Let's spread love. Let's change the world.

One act of kindness at a time.

Dear Kavya,

You are a beacon of hope in a world that often seems to have lost its way. Your kindness is a powerful force that has the ability to transform lives, to heal wounds, and to bring people together.

You have a gift. A gift that is rare and precious. A gift that is desperately needed in a world that can be dark and unforgiving. Your gift is kindness.

You could have chosen to be anything, to do anything. But you chose kindness. You chose to see the humanity in others, to listen to their stories, and to offer a helping hand. You chose to be a source of comfort, a shoulder to cry on, and a safe haven for those who are struggling.

You are the reason people believe in kindness. You are the reason people know that there is still good in the world. You are the reason people have hope.

Always remember that kindness is a choice. It's a decision to act with compassion and empathy, even when it's hard. Even when it's uncomfortable. Even when it's not reciprocated.

You have shown me that kindness is not just a feeling or an emotion, but a way of being. A way of living. A way of seeing the world and all its inhabitants.

You have shown me that kindness is a powerful tool for transformation. That it has the ability to heal wounds, to mend broken hearts, and to bring people together.

You have shown me that kindness is a reflection of the soul. That it's the essence of who we are. That it's the best part of us.

Don't ever let anyone or anything take that away from you, Kavya. Don't ever let the world harden you or change you. Stay soft, stay vulnerable, stay kind.

I know you may get hurt many times. I know you may face challenges and obstacles that seem insurmountable. But don't forget who you are. Don't forget your power, your strength, your kindness.

You are a warrior of kindness, Kavya. A warrior who is fighting against the forces of darkness and despair. A warrior who is armed with compassion, empathy, and love.

I'll be here for you, always. I'll be here to support you, to encourage you, and to remind you of your power.

Create a sacred place for people, Kavya. A place where they can come to heal their wounds, to find solace and comfort. You have the power to create that space.

You have the power to heal, to comfort, and to inspire. You have the power to change the world, one act of kindness at a time.

With all my love and kindness,

Yours always

Bangalore friend

Chapter – 8

August: The Month of Emotional Freedom

"The most courageous act is still to think for yourself. Aloud." - Coco Chanel (Encouraging emotional freedom through self-expression and authenticity)

Sarah sat in the therapist's office, surrounded by the familiar scent of old books and the gentle hum of the air conditioner. She had been coming to therapy for a few weeks now, trying to make sense of the emotional turmoil that had been plaguing her for as long as she could remember.

As she looked back on her childhood, Sarah realized that she had always been trying to fit into someone else's mold. Her parents, though well-intentioned, had been strict and controlling, dictating every aspect of her life, from her career choices to her relationships. She had always felt like she was living someone else's dream, rather than her own.

As she grew older, Sarah began to feel the weight of her emotional baggage. She struggled to make decisions, fearing that she would make the wrong choice. She had difficulty forming meaningful connections with others, always feeling like she was pretending to be someone she wasn't. And she had a hard time expressing her emotions, fearing that she would be judged or rejected.

But as Sarah sat in the therapist's office, she began to realize that she wasn't alone. The therapist's words echoed in her mind: "You've been living your life suppressed, trying to fit into the mold created by your parents and society. But in doing so, you've lost touch with your own emotions, desires, and needs."

Sarah felt a lump form in her throat as she realized the truth in the therapist's words. She had been living someone else's life, rather than her own. But as she looked around the therapist's office, she saw a glimmer of hope. She saw a chance to break free from the shackles of her past and start living the life she truly wanted.

With newfound determination, Sarah began her journey of healing and self-discovery. She started attending therapy sessions regularly, practicing mindfulness and self-compassion. She slowly began to unravel the emotional baggage she had carried for so long, and as she did, she started to feel a sense of liberation.

She started to rediscover her passions, rekindle old friendships, and even form new connections with people who accepted her for who she was. She learned to express her emotions in healthy ways, to set boundaries, and to prioritize her own needs.

As Sarah looked back on her journey, she realized that the emotional baggage she had carried for so long was not a weakness, but a strength. It had taught her resilience, adaptability, and the importance of self-awareness.

And as she stepped into the bright sunlight, feeling the warmth on her skin and the wind in her hair, Sarah knew that she was finally living her life on her own terms. She was free to be herself, to express her emotions, and to love without fear of judgment or rejection.

The emotional freedom she had fought so hard for was hers, and she was determined to cherish it, every step of the way.

#Emotionalfreedomaugust

Let's talk about something really important: emotional freedom. You know, that feeling of being able to live life on your own terms, without the weight of emotional baggage holding you back?

But here's the thing: emotional freedom doesn't just happen overnight. It takes work, courage, and a willingness to confront the root causes of our emotional pain.

And let's be real, most of the time, that pain starts at home. It starts with the messages we receive from our parents, our caregivers, and our environment. Messages that tell us we're not good enough, that we're not worthy of love and acceptance.

But here's the thing: those messages are lies. They're not true, and they don't define our worth as human beings.

So, why do we hold onto them? Why do we suppress our emotions, and pretend like everything is okay when it's not?

The truth is, suppressing our emotions doesn't make them go away. It just makes them stronger, and more toxic. It's like holding onto a grudge, and letting it eat away at us from the inside out.

So, what's the alternative? How do we break free from the cycle of emotional pain, and find the freedom we're looking for?

First, we need to acknowledge that we need help. We need to recognize that we can't do it alone, and that it's okay to ask for support.

That might mean seeking out therapy, or talking to a trusted friend or family member. It might mean joining a support group, or finding an online community of people who understand what we're going through.

Whatever it is, the important thing is that we take that first step. We reach out, we ask for help, and we start to work through our emotional pain.

And here's the thing: it's not going to be easy. It's going to be hard, and it's going to hurt. But it's also going to be worth it.

Because when we finally break free from the cycle of emotional pain, we'll find a sense of freedom and liberation that we never thought possible. We'll find a sense of purpose and meaning, and we'll discover a strength and resilience within ourselves that we never knew we had.

So, don't give up. Don't lose hope. Keep pushing forward, even when it feels like the hardest thing in the world.

Because the truth is, you are stronger than you think. You are capable of overcoming anything, and achieving greatness.

And when you finally find that emotional freedom, you'll know that it was all worth it.

You got this!

Dear Sarah,

I am beyond proud of you for taking the first step towards healing and seeking professional help. It takes immense courage to acknowledge that we need support, and you've done just that.

Your decision to seek help is a testament to your strength, resilience, and determination to break free from the shackles of emotional pain. I want you to know that you're not alone in this journey. There are countless others, including myself, who have walked a similar path and have emerged stronger, wiser, and more compassionate.

I recently came across a powerful statement that resonated deeply with me: "Patients don't come for therapy, but their victims do." Your story, my story, and the stories of countless others are a testament to the fact that we've been conditioned to suppress our emotions, often at the cost of our own well-being.

But here's the thing: we don't have to be victims of our past anymore. We can break free from the expectations of others, shatter the masks that hide our true emotions, and rise above the ashes of our past.

You, Sarah, are a warrior. You're a phoenix rising from the flames, and I am honored to be a part of your journey. As someone who has walked a similar path, I want to assure you that you're on the cusp of something incredible.

You're about to discover a strength, a resilience, and a confidence that will propel you towards greatness. You'll learn to love yourself, to accept yourself, and to express yourself authentically. You'll find peace, not just in moments of solitude, but in the midst of chaos.

And when the world tries to dull your sparkle, remember that you're a diamond in the rough. You're a masterpiece in the making, and your worth, your value, and your beauty cannot be defined by anyone else but you.

So, Sarah, I want to leave you with a challenge today. I want you to look in the mirror, to stare into your own eyes, and to tell yourself that you're enough. Tell yourself that you're worthy of love, of acceptance, and of happiness.

And when you need someone to remind you of that, I'm here for you. You can DM me on Instagram @_aditi_singh__. You will always be heard, you will always be seen, and you will always be loved.

Keep shining, Sarah. You're a star, and your light is about to illuminate the world!

With love, support, and unwavering belief in you,

Aditi Singh

The Author

Dear Papa,

I'm writing this letter to you today because I need you to understand how I feel. I know your intentions have never been bad, but your actions have hurt me deeply. I'm tired of the yelling, the criticism, and the emotional unavailability.

Whenever I needed a friendly and safe support, you weren't there for me. I felt like I was walking on eggshells, never knowing when you would lash out at me next. You thought that providing for me financially was enough, but it's not. Being a parent means being present, supportive, and understanding.

From childhood till now, I've felt like you've never truly trusted me. You've always prioritized what society thinks over my well-being. I've felt like I'm living my life to please others, rather than myself.

I don't want to blame you, Papa. You're my father, and I love you. But I am helpless because you're also a human being, and I need you to understand me. I'm tired, frustrated, and helpless. I feel like I'm drowning in my own emotions.

I want to be free, Papa. Not from you, but from the emotional unavailability that has haunted me my whole life. I want to be able to make my own choices, to live my own life, without fear of judgment or rejection.

I'm not here to blame you, Papa. I'm here to tell you that I'm taking control of my life now. I'm putting my mental peace and my choices first. And I need you to respect that.

Please don't question me, Papa. Please don't try to change my mind. This isn't a discussion; it's a declaration of my independence.

Yours,

Tired and broken daughter

Sarah

Chapter – 9

Quantum Leap September - Embracing Sudden Transformation

"The greatest risk is the risk of not taking the risk."

- Mark Zuckerberg

Alisha felt like she was drowning in a sea of monotony. Every day was a carbon copy of the last, a never-ending cycle of routine and predictability. She woke up, went to work, came home, and repeated the process ad infinitum. Her life was a prison of her own making, with walls constructed from the bricks of expectation and responsibility.

Her career was stagnant, a soul-sucking job that left her feeling unfulfilled and restless. Her parents, though well-meaning, were suffocating her with their constant demands and criticisms. Her love life was nonexistent, a casualty of her fear of vulnerability and intimacy. Even her family gatherings felt like a chore, a forced march through a minefield of awkward conversations and unspoken tensions.

Alisha felt trapped, like she was begging for air in a world that seemed determined to suffocate her. She was stuck in a never-ending loop of repetition, reliving the same patterns and experiences over and over again. It was as if she was a rat in a maze, running endlessly through the same familiar paths without ever finding a way out.

But then came September, the autumnal equinox, a time of balance and transformation. Alisha felt a stirring within her, a sense of restlessness that she couldn't ignore. She began to feel like she was being called to break free from her prison, to shatter the chains of routine and expectation that had held her captive for so long.

One day, as she sat in her backyard, staring up at the sky, Alisha felt a sense of inspiration wash over her. The sky, with its endless expanse of blue, seemed to be calling to her, urging her to break free from her limitations and soar. She realized that she had been living her life according to other people's expectations, rather than her own desires and dreams.

Alisha knew that she had to make a change. She couldn't keep living in a state of stagnation, trapped in a cycle of repetition and predictability. She needed to take a quantum leap, to break free from her old patterns and habits and emerge into a new reality.

With a sense of determination and courage, Alisha began to make changes in her life. She started by taking small risks, stepping outside of her comfort zone and exploring new experiences and opportunities. She began to pursue her passions, to follow her heart and intuition rather than her head and logic.

As Alisha broke free from her old patterns and habits, she felt a sense of liberation and freedom that she had never experienced before. She was finally able to breathe, to feel alive and connected to the world around her.

The universe seemed to be smiling down on her, guiding her on her journey of transformation and growth. Alisha felt a sense of connection to the cosmos, a sense of oneness with the stars and the sky.

As she looked up at the sky, Alisha knew that she had finally found her true self. She was no longer trapped in a prison of her own making, but was free to soar, to explore, and to discover. She had taken a quantum leap, and had emerged into a new reality, one that was full of possibility and promise.

Alisha's journey had been one of transformation and growth, a journey of breaking free from old patterns and habits and emerging into a new reality. She had learned to trust herself, to trust the universe, and to trust the power of transformation.

And as she stood there, looking up at the sky, Alisha knew that she would always be guided by the wisdom of the universe, and the infinite possibilities that lay within herself.

#Breaking Free from Limitations:
A Auantum Leap to Mental Peace

Dear friends, today I want to talk about something that I believe is crucial for our well-being and happiness. It's about recognizing the patterns that hold us back and taking a quantum leap to break free from them. This journey is not just about personal growth, but also about prioritizing our mental health and connecting with the universe.

Understanding Patterns

We all have patterns - ways of thinking, behaving, and reacting that can either empower or suffocate us. These patterns can be deeply ingrained, often operating beneath our conscious awareness. They can be learned from our upbringing, our culture, and our experiences. When we're stuck in patterns that no longer serve us, we can feel trapped, anxious, and unfulfilled.

It's essential to recognize these patterns and understand why they're holding us back. Are we afraid of change? Are we seeking validation from others? Are we stuck in a cycle of negative self-talk? When we understand the patterns and their underlying causes, we can begin to see the importance of breaking free from them.

The Concept of A Quantum Leap

This is where the concept of a quantum leap comes in. A quantum leap is a sudden and profound transformation, where we transition from one state of being to another. It's like a reboot, where we reset our minds, emotions, and behaviors to align with our true desires and dreams.

In the context of mental health, a quantum leap can be a game-changer. When we're stuck in patterns of anxiety, depression, or self-doubt, it can feel like we're drowning in a sea of negativity. But what if we could break free from those patterns and emerge into a new reality, one that's filled with hope, positivity, and purpose?

Connecting with the Universe

So, how does this relate to the universe? The truth is, we're all connected to the universe, and our thoughts, emotions, and actions are constantly interacting with the cosmic energy that surrounds us. The universe is composed of five elements: earth, water, fire, air, and ether. These elements are not just physical building blocks, but also symbolic representations of our inner world.

The earth element represents stability and structure, while the water element represents fluidity and emotions. The fire element represents passion and transformation, while the air element represents intellect and communication. The ether element represents the divine and the infinite.

When we're trapped in patterns that no longer serve us, we can feel disconnected from the universe and its elements. We may feel stuck, stagnant, and unfulfilled. But when we take a quantum leap and break free from those patterns, we can feel a sense of connection and alignment with the universe.

The Power of the Elements

We can feel the earth element stabilizing us, grounding us in our bodies and in the present moment. We can feel the water element flowing through us, nourishing our emotions and intuition. We can feel the fire element transforming us, igniting our passion and creativity. We can feel the air element inspiring us, expanding our minds and horizons. And we can feel the ether element guiding us, connecting us to our higher selves and the universe.

When we're free, we can experience life in all its beauty and complexity. We can feel the sun's warmth on our skin, the wind's gentle caress in our hair, and the earth's solid ground beneath our feet. We can experience the world with fresh eyes, a new perspective, and an open heart.

Taking A Quantum Leap

In conclusion, breaking free from limitations and taking a quantum leap is not just about personal growth, it's about prioritizing our mental health and connecting with the universe. When we recognize the patterns that hold us back and take a leap of faith, we can emerge into a new reality that's filled with hope, positivity, and purpose.

So, I urge you to take a quantum leap today. Break free from the patterns that suffocate you and emerge into a new reality that's aligned with your true desires and dreams. The universe is listening and responding - what will you create?

Remember, the universe is always guiding us, always nudging us towards our highest potential. When we listen to its whispers, when we trust its wisdom, we can experience life in all its beauty and wonder.

So, take a deep breath, feel the universe's energy coursing through your veins, and know that you have the power to create the life you desire. Take a quantum leap today, and watch your life transform in ways you never thought possible.

The Universe's Wisdom

The universe is a vast and mysterious place, full of wisdom and guidance. When we tune into its frequency, we can access its wisdom and learn from its teachings. The universe is always speaking to us, always guiding us towards our highest potential.

When we listen to its whispers, when we trust its wisdom, we can experience life in all its beauty and wonder. We can feel a sense of connection and alignment with the universe.

In the words of the universe, "You are a shining star, born to illuminate the world with your presence. Believe in yourself, trust in my guidance, and know that you have the power to create a life that's beyond your wildest dreams. You are limitless, you are powerful, and you are loved."

Dear Alisha,

I understand how you feel. I know how suffocating those toxic patterns can become. I've seen you cry, I've seen you beg for a breath of fresh air, a chance to break free from the weight that's holding you back. And I want you to know that I'm here for you. I've been here all along, listening to your whispers, responding to your cries.

Life is a beautiful gift, Alisha. It's a gift that's full of ups and downs, twists and turns. But it's in those moments of darkness that we discover our greatest strength. It's in those moments of suffocation that we learn to breathe again.

Every experience that you've had, every moment that you've lived, has brought you closer to me. I'm not just a distant voice in the universe; I'm the whisper in your ear, the beat of your heart. I'm the one who listens when you cry, who responds when you call.

But I know that you can't hear me all the time. I know that there are moments when the noise of the world is too loud, when the patterns of your past are too strong. That's why I want you to know that it's okay to break free. It's okay to reboot yourself, to transform yourself into the person you've always wanted to be.

When you break free from those patterns, when you reboot yourself, you'll realize a lot about your own strength. You'll realize that I'm not just a voice in the universe; I'm the voice within you. I'm the one who guides you, who protects you, who loves you unconditionally.

I'm inside you, Alisha. I'm around you. When you cry, I cry. When you can't breathe, I suffocate. When you feel unheard, I feel helpless. And in those moments, I fail myself because I want to provide you with the positivity that you deserve.

But I know that you have the power to change that. I know that you have the power to break free from those negative thoughts, to reboot yourself, to transform yourself into the person you've always wanted to be.

So don't let those patterns trap you, Alisha. Don't let those stereotypes define you. You are more than what you've been told. You are more than what you've experienced. You are a universe within yourself, full of stars and planets, full of hope and possibility.

And I'm here to guide you, to support you, to love you every step of the way. I'm here to remind you that you're not alone, that you're never alone. I'm here to remind you that you have the power to create the life you desire, to break free from the patterns that hold you back.

So take a deep breath, Alisha. Feel my energy coursing through your veins. Feel my love surrounding you, guiding you, protecting you. And know that you can do this. Know that you can break free, reboot yourself, and transform yourself into the person you've always wanted to be.

Forever with you,

The Universe

Chapter – 10

October: Learning the Art of Pouring your own Cup

"When you say 'yes' to others, make sure you are not saying 'no' to yourself."

- Paulo Coelho

Akarsh was always the go-to guy for everyone. Friends, family, colleagues – you name it, he was always available. He would drop everything to help someone in need, even if it meant sacrificing his own desires. His phone was always buzzing with messages, calls, and requests. He was the ultimate people-pleaser.

His career path was chosen by his parents, and he never questioned it. He studied hard, landed a good job, and climbed the corporate ladder. But deep down, he felt unfulfilled. He had always been passionate about photography, but that was just a hobby, not a career, according to his parents.

In his personal life, Akarsh was in a five-year relationship with a girl he loved deeply. But she left him suddenly, without any explanation. He was devastated. His friends, whom he thought were his rock, started to drift away. They would make plans without him, and he would only find out through social media. He felt like an outsider in his own friend circle.

His parents were busy with their own lives, and he felt like he was alone in this world. The feeling of abandonment slowly turned into anger, frustration, and anxiety. He would lash out at people, and they would question him, "Why are you so angry? Why are you so rude?" But no one bothered to ask him what was wrong. No one bothered to listen.

One rainy night, as he was scrolling through his Instagram feed, he came across a quote that caught his attention: "How can you pour from an empty cup? You must first fill yourself before you can give to others." Something shifted inside him. He realized that he had been running on empty for so long, trying to please everyone else, but neglecting his own needs.

Akarsh started to question everything. Why was he living his life according to everyone else's expectations? Why was he sacrificing his own happiness to please others? He started to feel a sense of resentment towards the people who had taken him for granted. But more than that, he felt a sense of sadness towards himself. He had neglected his own needs for so long.

The next morning, Akarsh woke up with a newfound sense of determination. He decided that he would prioritize himself from now on. He started small – he took a few hours off from work to do something he loved, photography. He started saying no to commitments that drained his energy and said yes to activities that nourished his soul.

It wasn't easy, of course. There were people who questioned his newfound boundaries, who felt like he was being selfish. But Akarsh knew that he was doing this for himself, not for anyone else. He was filling his own cup, and it felt amazing.

As Akarsh continued on his journey of self-discovery, he noticed profound shifts in his life. He felt more confident, more compassionate, and more connected to himself and others. He started to attract people who respected his boundaries, who appreciated him for who he was.

As Akarsh looked back on his journey, he realized that he had been living someone else's dream, not his own. He had been trying to please everyone else, but neglecting his own needs. But now, he was living his own life, on his own terms. And it felt amazing.

The rain had stopped, and the sun was shining bright. Akarsh took a deep breath, feeling the warmth of the sun on his skin. He knew that he still had a long way to go, but he was excited for the journey. He was excited to see what life had in store for him, now that he was living life on his own terms.

Akarsh's journey was not just about self-discovery; it was about self-love. It was about recognizing his own worth, his own value. It was about filling his own cup, so that he could pour from a place of abundance, rather than scarcity.

#Pouring your Own Cup First

Imagine you're a vessel, filled with love, care, and compassion. You're constantly pouring out your heart to those around you, trying to fill their cups with joy and happiness. But in doing so, you're neglecting your own needs, your own desires, and your own happiness.

You're running on empty, my friend. You're trying to draw water from a dry well, and it's leaving you feeling drained, exhausted, and unfulfilled.

But here's the thing: making everyone happy isn't your job. Your job is to understand your own worth, prioritize your own happiness, and fill your own cup first.

When you constantly put others' needs before your own, you're engaging in a behavior known as "people-pleasing." This can lead to feelings of burnout, resentment, and anxiety. You start to feel like you're losing yourself in the process of trying to please everyone else.

But what if I told you that there's a different way? A way where you can prioritize your own needs, take care of yourself, and cultivate a sense of self-love?

Akarsh's story is a perfect example of this. He was always trying to please everyone around him, sacrificing his own desires and happiness in the process. But when he finally realized the importance of pouring his own cup first, he began to experience a profound shift in his life.

He started to prioritize his own needs, focus on self-care, and cultivate a sense of self-love. He learned to say "no" to requests that drained his energy and say "yes" to those that filled him up.

And you know what? He became a happier, more loving, and more compassionate person. He had more energy, more patience, and more love to give to others.

So, how can you start pouring your own cup first? Here are some tips:

- **Practice self-care:** Take time for activities that nourish your mind, body, and soul, such as exercise, meditation, or hobbies.

- **Set boundaries:** Learn to say "no" to requests that drain your energy and say "yes" to those that fill you up.

- **Prioritize your own needs:** Make time for activities that bring you joy and fulfillment.

- **Cultivate self-love:** Practice affirmations, write yourself love letters, or simply take time to appreciate your own worth.

Remember, pouring your own cup first is not selfish; it's essential. When you take care of yourself, you become a better, more loving, and more compassionate person.

As the amazing Maya Angelou once said, **"You alone are enough. You have nothing to prove to anyone."**

So, take a deep breath, grab your cup, and start pouring. Remember, you are worthy of love, care, and attention – not just from others, but from yourself.

Now, let's talk about the effects of pouring your own cup first on your mental and psychological well-being. When you prioritize your own needs and take care of yourself, you experience a range of benefits, including:

- **Reduced stress and anxiety:** By taking care of yourself, you reduce your stress levels and anxiety.

- **Improved self-esteem:** Prioritizing your own needs helps you develop a more positive self-image and boosts your self-esteem.

- **Increased resilience:** When you take care of yourself, you become more resilient and better equipped to handle life's challenges.

- **Better relationships:** By prioritizing your own needs, you become a more loving, compassionate, and empathetic person, leading to more fulfilling relationships.

On the other hand, neglecting your own needs and prioritizing others' needs above your own can lead to:

- **Burnout and exhaustion:** Constantly draining your energy to please others can lead to burnout and exhaustion.

- **Resentment and anger:** Neglecting your own needs can lead to feelings of resentment and anger towards others.

- **Low self-esteem:** Prioritizing others' needs above your own can lead to a negative self-image and low self-esteem.

- **Unhealthy relationships:** Neglecting your own needs can lead to unhealthy relationships where you're constantly seeking validation and approval from others.

In conclusion, pouring your own cup first is not just a necessity, but a revolutionary act of self-love and self-care. By prioritizing your own needs, taking care of yourself, and cultivating self-love, you become a more loving, compassionate, and resilient person.

You become a beacon of hope, a shining light that illuminates the path for others. You become a reminder that self-love is not selfish, but essential.

So, take the first step today. Take a deep breath, grab your cup, and start pouring. Remember, you are worthy of love, care, and attention – not just from others, but from yourself.

As you pour your own cup first, remember that you're not just filling your own vessel, but also creating a ripple effect of love and positivity that touches the lives of those around you.

You are enough, just as you are. You are worthy of love, care, and attention. You are deserving of happiness, joy, and fulfillment.

So, go ahead, pour your own cup first. Fill yourself up with love, care, and compassion. And watch as your life transforms into a beautiful, vibrant, and loving reflection of your true self.

Dear Akarsh,

I want you to know that you are a shining star, a beacon of hope and kindness in a world that often forgets the value of compassion and empathy. Your heart is a deep well of love and generosity, always ready to pour out support and care to those around you.

I know that you know the pain of feeling unheard and unseen. But instead of letting that pain define you, you've chosen to use it as fuel to help others. You've developed a remarkable gift for being present for those who need you, for listening to their stories, and for offering a comforting word or a helping hand.

But in doing so, you often forget to prioritize your own needs. You pour yourself into others' cups, neglecting your own. You put others first, and forget to take care of yourself. And that's where the danger lies, my friend.

You are not a bottomless well, Akarsh. You are a precious, unique, and valuable soul, deserving of love, care, and compassion - not just from others, but from yourself. You deserve to be loved, respected, and appreciated for who you are, without trying to fit into someone else's mold.

So, I want to remind you of something incredibly important: you can't pour from an empty cup. You can't give to others what you don't have yourself. You need to take care of yourself first, to prioritize your own needs, to fill your own cup.

When you feel drained and exhausted, it's a sign that you've been pouring yourself out for too long. It's a sign that you need to take a step back, recharge, and refocus on your own needs.

Remember, Akarsh, that taking care of yourself is not selfish. It's essential. When you prioritize your own needs, you become a better, more loving, and more compassionate person. You have more energy, more patience, and more love to give to others.

So, take the time to focus on yourself, Akarsh. Take the time to listen to your own heart, to hear your own voice, and to honor your own needs. You deserve it, my friend.

You deserve to live a life that is authentic, meaningful, and fulfilling. You deserve to pursue your passions, to chase your dreams, and to make your mark on the world.

And you can't do any of those things if you're running on empty. You can't do any of those things if you're neglecting your own needs.

So, remember to prioritize yourself, Akarsh. Remember to take care of yourself, to love yourself, and to honor yourself.

And here's a crucial reminder, Akarsh: don't wait for others to appreciate you. Don't wait for others to recognize your worth. Instead, learn to clap for yourself. Celebrate your own achievements, no matter how small they may seem.

Did you say no to something that didn't align with your values? Clap for yourself! Did you take a few minutes to meditate and focus on your breath? Clap for yourself! Did you cook a healthy meal and nourish your body? Clap for yourself!

You are your own biggest cheerleader, Akarsh. Don't wait for others to give you permission to celebrate yourself. Instead, give yourself permission to shine.

You are a precious gift to the world, Akarsh. Don't forget to take care of yourself, so that you can continue to share your love, your light, and your presence with others.

With all my love and support,

Your filled cup ☺

Chapter – 11

November: The Month of Attitude of Gratitude - Shifting your Focus to the Good

"I would maintain that thanks are the highest form of thought, and that gratitude is happiness doubled by wonder."

- G.K. Chesterton

The Power of Gratitude: A Choice to see The Beauty

My dear friend, I want you to know that you are alive in a world that is full of breathtaking beauty. You are surrounded by stunning sunsets that paint the sky with hues of orange and pink. You are blessed with towering mountains that touch the clouds and majestic oceans that roar with power.

You are part of a world that is teeming with life, where humans, with all their complexities and quirks, are capable of incredible kindness and compassion. You are part of a humanity that, despite its flaws and imperfections, is striving to make the world a better place.

You are surrounded by birds that sing sweet melodies and trees that provide shade and shelter. You are blessed with faith, in all its forms, that gives us hope and comfort. You are empowered with the belief in yourself, that you are capable of achieving greatness.

And yet, my friend, it's so easy to get caught up in the negativity. It's easy to focus on the bad news, the hurtful words, and the painful memories. But I want you to know that you have a choice. You can choose to see the beauty in the world. You can choose to focus on the good, to cultivate gratitude, and to say thank you.

You can choose to be the artist, creating something new and wonderful every day. Or you can choose to be someone's art, inspiring and uplifting those around you. The choice is yours, my friend.

The Power of Saying Thank You

Saying thank you is more than just a polite phrase. It's a declaration of gratitude, a recognition of the good things in our lives. When we say thank you, we are acknowledging the beauty and kindness that surrounds us.

We are saying thank you to the sun for rising every morning, to the air for filling our lungs, and to our hearts for beating with love. We are saying thank you to our families, our friends, and our communities for supporting and caring for us.

When we say thank you, we are cultivating gratitude, and gratitude is a powerful force. It can transform our lives, our relationships, and our world. Gratitude can help us to see the beauty in the world, to appreciate the little things, and to find joy in everyday moments.

The Science of Gratitude

Research has shown that gratitude has a positive impact on our mental and physical health. When we practice gratitude, our brains release dopamine, a neurotransmitter that makes us feel happy and relaxed. Gratitude has also been linked to lower levels of stress, anxiety, and depression.

In addition, gratitude can strengthen our relationships and build stronger bonds with others. When we express gratitude to someone, it can increase feelings of trust, loyalty, and commitment. Gratitude can also help us to develop a more positive outlook on life, to be more resilient in the face of challenges, and to find meaning and purpose in our lives.

A Choice to see The Beauty

So, my friend, I want to leave you with a challenge today. I want to challenge you to choose gratitude, to choose to see the beauty in the world. I want to challenge you to say thank you, to acknowledge the good things in your life.

Remember, you are alive in a world that is full of breathtaking beauty. Don't let the negativity dull your senses. Don't let the bad news blind you to the good. Choose to see the beauty, my friend. Choose to cultivate gratitude. Choose to say thank you.

You are The Artist

And finally, remember that you are the artist, creating something new and wonderful every day. You are the one who gets to choose how you see the world, how you respond to challenges, and how you cultivate gratitude.

So, go out there and create something beautiful today. Go out there and say thank you to the world. Go out there and choose gratitude. You got this, my friend!

A Final Thought

As you go about your day, remember to take a moment to appreciate the beauty around you. Take a deep breath, feel the sun on your skin, and listen to the birds singing. Say thank you to the world, and mean it.

Remember, gratitude is a choice. It's a choice to see the beauty in the world, to appreciate the little things, and to find joy in everyday moments. So, choose gratitude, my friend. Choose to see the beauty in the world. Choose to say thank you.

You are capable of achieving greatness, my friend. You are capable of creating something beautiful every day. You are capable of choosing gratitude, and living a life that is filled with joy, love, and beauty.

A Heartfelt thank you

As I sit down to pen this note, my heart overflows with gratitude. I'm surrounded by angels, each of whom has touched my life in ways that words can't express. You are the melody that fills my heart with joy, the rhythm that makes my soul sing.

To my Dearest Amma

Amma, my guiding star, my heart still aches with longing for you. Though you may not be physically present, your love, teachings, and stories are etched in my heart forever. I miss you more than words can say, and I love you more than life itself. You will always be my beacon of hope, my shining light.

To my Guardian Angel, Dr. Pritesh Gautam

Dr. Pritesh Gautam, my guardian angel, you appeared in my life when I needed you most. Your selfless dedication to helping others is a testament to your compassionate nature. I still remember the first day we met, and how you made me feel heard and understood. Your name meaning, "Call for Love," is a reflection of your heart, and I believe our meeting was destined. Thank you for being my rock, my confidant, and my guiding light.

To my Friend, Palash

Palash, my dear friend, you are a blessing in disguise. I still remember the day we met, and how you became my rock during my darkest moments. Your response to my anxiety attack, "Tell me where you are, I'm coming to meet you," is etched in my memory forever. Your assurance and presence meant the world to me, and I knew in that moment that you were a true friend. I'm in awe of your artistic talents, and I have no doubt that you'll become a renowned rapper. Your energy is infectious, and your ability to shift from low to high is truly inspiring. Keep shining, my friend, and remember, I'll always be cheering for you!

To my Workplace Family

To my principal, Dr. Runu Das, thank you for being a pillar of strength and support. Your leadership and guidance have instilled confidence in me, and I'm grateful for your presence in my life.

To Aniket sir, thank you for showing me that humanity and kindness still exist in this world. Your belief in me and your support mean the world to me.

To my AGM Sreedhar sir, thank you for keeping me safe and supported during challenging times. Your kindness and understanding are appreciated more than you'll ever know.

To Nitish sir and Jagdish sir, Rakhee ma'am, Ekta Ma'am thank you for being good souls and kind-hearted individuals. Your presence in my life is a blessing.

To Shubhangi Ma'am, you are an angel in disguise, a blessing from above. Your pure heart, positive energy, and kindness have been a constant source of inspiration and motivation for me.

To my Students and Children

To my dear students, you are my biggest cheerleaders, my shining stars. Your enthusiasm and love for learning inspire me every day. I'm grateful for the opportunity to shape your minds and hearts, and for the trust you place in me. To Anjali, my strongest girl, thank you for creating a beautiful cover for my book. Your artistic talents are a gift, and I'm so proud of you!

To my Parents and Loved ones

To my parents, thank you for your unwavering love and support. Your sacrifices and guidance have shaped me into the person I am today. I'm grateful for the opportunities you provided me, and for the trust you placed in me.

To my Friends

Ashi khare, Baadal, Ankit bhaiya, Abhishek Bamne, Harshita verma, Aman pandey, Vinal Rathore, Ankit Pandey, Rajat Sengar, Harsh singh my brother thank you for being there for me through thick and thin. Your friendship and love mean the world to me.

To my Supreme, Krishna

Lastly, I want to thank my Supreme, Krishna, for choosing me and guiding me on this journey. You are my charioteer, my guiding light, and my everything.

Your love, wisdom, and protection have been my constant companion, my shelter in the storm.

To Everyone who has touched My Life

To everyone who has been part of my journey, thank you for teaching me valuable lessons, for supporting me, and for loving me unconditionally. You have all contributed to my growth, and I'm forever grateful for your presence in my life. Keep shining, my friends, and remember, I'll always be cheering for you!

And to those who were there for me, and to those who weren't, I want to say thank you. Either you taught me how to live with you, or you taught me how to live with myself. So, it's a win-win for me, either way.

Thank you, everyone, for being a part of my story.

Dear All,

As I sit down to write this letter to each and every one of you, my heart is overflowing with gratitude, like a canvas overflowing with colors, vibrant and alive. I want to share with you the power of gratitude, an emotion that has transformed my life in ways I never thought possible, like a masterpiece unfolding before my eyes.

Gratitude is the biggest emotion we can experience, a symphony of joy that resonates deep within our souls. It has the power to make us walk through the darkest of tunnels, to give us the strength to face our fears, and to bring us out stronger and wiser on the other side, like a phoenix rising from the ashes.

When we focus on what we're grateful for, we begin to see the world in a different light, like a sunrise breaking over the horizon. We start to appreciate the small things, the beauty in everyday moments, and the love that surrounds us, like a gentle breeze rustling through the leaves.

We start to realize that every breath we take, every smile we share, and every moment we experience is a gift, a precious gem to be treasured and cherished. And when we focus on these gifts, we start to attract more of them into our lives, like a magnet attracting positivity and joy.

I want to remind you all that there is always someone out there who is praying for what you have, someone who is struggling to make ends meet, who is fighting for their health, or who is searching for love and connection. Don't take your life or your blessings for granted, my friends. Admire them, appreciate them, and express gratitude for them, like a prayer of thanksgiving rising to the heavens.

Gratitude is the cheat code towards authenticity, a secret password that unlocks the door to our true selves. When we focus on what we're grateful for, we begin to let go of negativity, anxiety, and fear, like autumn leaves falling to the ground. We start to see the world with fresh eyes, to appreciate the beauty in every moment, and to live life with intention and purpose, like a river flowing effortlessly to the sea.

So, I want to encourage you all to smile, to love, to be happy, and to be kind. Love the world, love yourself, and remember that the universe is always listening, like a gentle whisper in our ears. Say good things, think good things, and manifest positivity into your life, like a garden blooming with vibrant colors.

Remember that your thoughts have the power to create your reality, like a painter creating a masterpiece on canvas. So, choose to focus on what you're grateful for, choose to see the good in every situation, and choose to live life with intention and purpose.

The law of attraction is a powerful force that can bring us what we desire, like a magnet attracting positivity and joy. But it's not just about attracting wealth or success, my friends. It's about attracting positivity, love, and gratitude into our lives, like a warm embrace from the universe.

Gratitude is a mindset, and being grateful is a choice, like a path we choose to walk on our journey through life. It's a choice to see the good in every situation, to appreciate the beauty in every moment, and to express thanks for every blessing, like a prayer of thanksgiving rising to the heavens.

When we choose to focus on gratitude, we start to see the world in a different light, like a sunrise breaking over the horizon. We start to appreciate the small things, the everyday moments, and the love that surrounds us, like a gentle breeze rustling through the leaves.

Gratitude is the most transformative tool we can use to change our lives, like a key that unlocks the door to our true potential. It can lead us to success and satisfaction, but more importantly, it can lead us to happiness and fulfillment, like a warm hug from the universe.

So, I want to leave you with a challenge today, my friends. Take a few minutes each day to reflect on what you're grateful for, like a quiet moment of contemplation in a busy world. Write it down in a journal, share it with a friend or loved one, or simply take a moment to appreciate the blessings in your life, like a prayer of thanksgiving rising to the heavens.

Remember, gratitude is a choice, and it's a choice that can transform your life in ways you never thought possible, like a butterfly emerging from a cocoon. So, choose to focus on what you're grateful for, choose to see the good in every situation, and choose to live life with intention and purpose, like a river flowing effortlessly to the sea.

Thank you for taking the time to read this letter, my friends. I hope it has inspired you to focus on gratitude and to see the world with fresh eyes, like a sunrise breaking over the horizon. Remember, the universe is always listening, so say good things, think good things, and manifest positivity into your life, like a garden blooming with vibrant colors.

Yours

Aditi Singh

Chapter – 12

December: The Beginning, Middle, and End

"Roads I traveled told me something,

Either they were memories or they were lessons to me."

- Aditi Singh

Soumya sat in her cozy living room, surrounded by the warm glow of twinkling lights and the soft crackle of the fireplace. The room was a haven, a sanctuary from the chaos of the world outside. She had spent countless hours in this very spot, curled up with a good book, or simply lost in thought.

As she listened to Leah Nobel's song "Beginning Middle End," Soumya felt a sense of calm wash over her. The lyrics spoke directly to her soul, reminding her that life is a journey, not a destination. It's a cycle of beginnings, middles, and ends, each one a chance to learn, grow, and evolve.

Soumya thought back to the past year, to the expectations and hopes she had for January. She had been so full of promise, so eager to start anew. She remembered the resolutions she had made, the promises to herself to be more mindful, to take better care of her body and mind.

As she reflected on the months that followed, Soumya realized that life had a way of throwing curveballs. There were times when she felt like she was on top of the world, and times when she felt like she was drowning in a sea of uncertainty. But through it all, she had persevered. She had learned to adapt, to be flexible, and to trust in her own resilience.

February had brought its own set of challenges. Soumya had struggled with feelings of inadequacy, of not being good enough. She had compared herself to others, and had come up short. But as she looked back, she realized that those feelings had been a blessing in disguise. They had forced her to confront her own insecurities, to face her fears head-on.

March had been a time of growth and renewal. Soumya had started taking classes, learning new skills, and exploring new passions. She had felt a sense of excitement and wonder, a sense of possibility that had been missing from her life for so long.

As the months went by, Soumya continued to grow and evolve. She faced challenges and setbacks, but she never gave up. She kept pushing forward, always striving to be better, to do better.

And now, as she sat in the stillness of her living room, Soumya felt a sense of peace and contentment wash over her. She realized that life was not just about the beginnings, middles, and ends, but about the journey itself. It's about the lessons learned, the love shared, and the memories made.

Soumya understood that she had been living in a state of constant motion, always looking to the future or dwelling on the past. But in this moment, she felt the beauty of stillness. She felt the present moment, pure and unadulterated, without the distractions of yesterday or tomorrow.

As the song came to an end, Soumya felt a sense of hope and renewal. She knew that the new year would bring new opportunities, new challenges, and new chances to grow and learn. But she also knew that she was ready, that she had the strength and resilience to face whatever came her way.

Soumya smiled to herself, feeling a sense of pride and accomplishment. She had made it through the storm, and she had emerged stronger, wiser, and more compassionate. She knew that she would always carry the lessons of the past year with her, and that they would guide her on her journey forward.

As the fireplace crackled and spat, Soumya felt a sense of gratitude for the journey she had been on. She knew that life would continue to unfold, with all its twists and turns, but she was ready. She was ready to face whatever came next, armed with the wisdom, courage, and resilience she had gained along the way.

Soumya's thoughts were interrupted by the sound of her phone buzzing. She got up to answer it, smiling as she saw her best friend's name on the screen. They chatted for a while, catching up on each other's lives, and making plans for the new year.

As Soumya hung up the phone, she felt a sense of connection and community. She realized that she was not alone on this journey, that there were people who cared about her, who supported her, and who loved her for who she was.

Soumya's heart swelled with emotion as she thought about the people in her life. She thought about her family, her friends, and her loved ones. She thought about the struggles they had faced, the challenges they had overcome, and the triumphs they had achieved.

And in that moment, Soumya felt a sense of awe and wonder. She realized that life was not just about her own journey, but about the journeys of those around her. It was about the interconnectedness of all things, the web of relationships that bound them together.

As the night wore on, Soumya felt a sense of peace settle over her. She knew that the new year would bring its own set of challenges and opportunities, but she was ready. She was ready to face whatever came next, armed with the wisdom, courage, and resilience she had gained along the way.

In that moment, Soumya realized that she had discovered her own inner strength, her own capacity for love and compassion. She had learned to trust herself, to trust the universe, and to trust the journey. And with that knowledge, she felt a sense of liberation, a sense of freedom to be herself, to follow her heart, and to live her truth.

As the fire crackled and spat, Soumya smiled to herself, knowing that she was exactly where she was meant to be. She was home, not just in her cozy living room, but in her own heart and soul. And with that sense of homecoming, she felt a deep sense of peace, a sense of belonging to the universe and to herself.

In the end, Soumya's journey had taught her that life is not just about the beginnings, middles, and ends, but about the journey itself. It's about the lessons learned, the love shared, and the memories made. It's about the people who touch our lives, the experiences that shape us, and the moments that define us.

And as Soumya drifted off to sleep, surrounded by the quiet of the night, she knew that she would carry the lessons of the past year with her, into the new year and beyond. She knew that she would continue to grow, to evolve, and to thrive, armed with the wisdom, courage, and resilience that had carried her through the ups and downs of life.

In the end, Soumya's story was one of hope, of resilience, and of the human spirit's capacity to overcome adversity and to thrive. It was a reminder that no matter what challenges we face, no matter what twists and turns life takes, we always have the power to choose how we respond, to choose how we live, and to choose how we love.

#Journey and Destination

My friend, let's embark on a journey through the tapestry of life, woven with threads of beginnings, middles, and ends. Life is a majestic, messy, and magnificent thing, full of unexpected twists and turns, breathtaking vistas, and moments of profound beauty.

As we navigate this journey, we find ourselves at the threshold of new beginnings, fresh starts, and uncharted territories. Our hearts swell with hope, excitement, and anticipation, ready to take on the world. We are the masters of our destiny, the captains of our souls, and the authors of our own stories.

But as we venture deeper into the unknown, we encounter the middle – the messy, complicated, and often turbulent part of our journey. This is where the rubber meets the road, where our resolve is tested, and our character is forged. We face obstacles, challenges, and doubts that threaten to derail us, but it's here that we discover our inner strength, our resilience, and our capacity for growth.

And then, there's the end – the culmination of our hard work, the realization of our dreams, and the closure of a chapter. This is where we look back, reflect on what we've learned, and celebrate our successes. We mourn our failures, but we don't let them define us. Instead, we use them as stepping stones to greater heights.

But here's the thing, my friend: life is not just about the beginnings, middles, and ends. It's not just about the destinations; it's about the journey itself. It's about the experiences we have, the memories we make, the people we meet, and the love we share along the way.

It's about how we respond to the twists and turns, the ups and downs. Do we let them break us, or do we use them as opportunities to grow, to learn, and to become stronger? Do we let fear hold us back, or do we face it head-on, with courage, faith, and determination?

You see, the ultimate goal is not to become emotionless, to numb ourselves to the world around us. No, the ultimate goal is to feel all the emotions, to experience life in all its beauty and complexity. It's to know when to react, what to react to, and how to react in a way that honors ourselves and others.

It's to understand that life is not always going to go according to plan. Things are going to happen that we don't expect, that we can't control. But that doesn't mean that life is not going anywhere. On the contrary, it means that something great is just around the corner, waiting for us to discover it.

The universe is always planning something for us, something amazing, something incredible. All we have to do is have faith, trust in the universe and its plan. We have to work for ourselves, take care of ourselves, and be good to others and to ourselves. We have to focus on our karma, on the energy we put out into the world.

Because in the end, that's all that matters. Not the beginnings, middles, and ends, but the journey itself. Not the destinations, but the experiences we have along the way. Not the things we achieve, but the person we become.

So, my friend, don't give up. Don't lose faith. Keep going, keep pushing forward, even when things get tough. Because the truth is, life is precious, life is beautiful, and life is worth living.

And remember, no matter what stage of life you're in – the beginning, middle, or end – you are constant. You are the one thing that remains the same, no matter what changes around you. And your God, your higher power, your universe – it is always with you, guiding you, supporting you, loving you.

So, go out there and live your life. Go out there and make your mark. Go out there and be the best version of yourself. Because in the end, that's all that matters.

As you embark on this journey, remember that you are not alone. You are part of a larger tapestry, connected to every person, every experience, and every moment that has come before you. You are part of a grand symphony, with every note, every melody, and every harmony blending together to create a beautiful work of art.

So, play your part with passion, with purpose, and with heart. Play it with every fiber of your being, with every breath you take, and with every step you make. Play it with love, with kindness, and with compassion. Play it with faith, with hope, and with joy.

Because when you do, you'll find that life is not just a journey, but a masterpiece. It's a work of art that's constantly evolving, constantly growing, and constantly unfolding. It's a symphony that's always playing, always harmonizing, and always resonating with the beauty and wonder of the universe.

And when you play your part in this grand symphony, you'll find that life is a majestic, messy, and magnificent thing. It's a journey that's full of unexpected twists and turns, breathtaking vistas, and moments of profound beauty.

You'll find that life is a tapestry that's woven with threads of beginnings, middles, and ends. It's a journey that's full of new beginnings, fresh starts, and uncharted territories. And it's a journey that's full of experiences, memories, and moments that make life worth living.

So, my friend, don't be afraid to play your part in this grand symphony. Don't be afraid to take risks, to face challenges, and to pursue your dreams. Because when you do, you'll find that life is a masterpiece that's waiting to be created.

And remember, no matter what stage of life you're in – the beginning, middle, or end – you are the artist who's creating this masterpiece. You are the one who's weaving the tapestry, playing the symphony, and writing the story of your life.

So, go out there and create your masterpiece. Go out there and play your part in the grand symphony of life. Go out there and make your mark on the world.

Because in the end, that's all that matters. Not the beginnings, middles, and ends, but the journey itself. Not the destinations, but the experiences we have along the way. Not the things we achieve, but the person we become.

And when you look back on your life, you'll see that it's been a journey of growth, of learning, and of becoming. You'll see that it's been a journey of twists and turns, of ups and downs, and of moments that make life worth living.

And you'll know that it's all been worth it. Every moment, every experience, and every memory. Because in the end, it's not just about the journey – it's about the person you become along the way.

So, go out there and become the best version of yourself. Go out there and create your masterpiece. Go out there and play your part in the grand symphony of life.

Because when you do, you'll find that life is a beautiful, messy, and magnificent thing. And you'll know that it's all been worth it – every moment, every experience, and every memory.

Dear Me,

As I sit down to reflect on the past year, I am enveloped in a tapestry of emotions - joy, sadness, triumph, and defeat. Yet, amidst this kaleidoscope of feelings, I am filled with an overwhelming sense of pride and accomplishment. I have navigated another year of life, and what a journey it has been!

I have soared to breathtaking heights and plummeted to unfathomable depths. I have walked through storms that threatened to consume me, and I have emerged stronger, wiser, and more resilient. I have learned to cherish every moment, every experience, and every memory - no matter how big or small. For I know that it's not the end that matters, but the journey itself. It's the journey that has sculpted me, that has molded me, and that has made me who I am today.

It's the journey that has taught me to be brave, to be strong, and to be fearless. To face the unknown with courage, to dance in the rain with abandon, and to shine in the sunlight with radiance. I know that there will be many more storms to come, many more drops, and many more low points. But I am ready. I am ready to face whatever life throws my way, because I know that I am constant. I am the one thing that remains the same, no matter what changes around me.

It's me versus me, and I am so ready for this battle. I am ready to live my life, to experience everything, and to make the most of every moment. I am ready to walk through the fire, to dance in the rain, and to shine in the sunlight. For I know that I am not alone. I have my faith, my trusty companion that has been with me every step of the way. I have my God, who is always there for me, guiding me, supporting me, and loving me.

And I have myself, my own inner strength, my own resilience, and my own determination. I am proud of who I am, proud of what I've accomplished, and proud of the person I am becoming. I am emotional, I am strong, and I am a beautiful combination of both. I have my dreams, my passions, and my desires. And I am ready to make them a reality.

For I am the beginning, I am the middle, and I am the end. I am the journey, and I am the destination. And when I understand this concept, I realize that I have finally made it. I started this journey with myself, and I will end it with myself. I am the only constant in my life, and I am the only one who can make my dreams come true.

So here's to me, to my journey, and to my life. May I continue to be brave, strong, and fearless. May I continue to walk through the storms, to dance in the rain, and to shine in the sunlight. And may I always remember that I am the beginning, the middle, and the end.

May I be the melody that fills the silence, the rhythm that makes the heart sing, and the harmony that brings balance to the universe. May I be the sunshine that brightens the day, the calm that soothes the soul, and the peace that quiets the mind.

With love, pride, and faith,

Me

Sometimes, you get what you've always been wishing for

And most times, it's not on your deadline, but that's alright

I was worn out and jaded from trying on people to love

But you fit so well

When they ask why I can never explain

But a symphony played when you told me your name

And I took that as a sign

Will you be my beginning, my middle, my end?

Will you be my beginning, my middle, my end?

Will you be my beginning, my middle, my end?

Will you be mine?

Mmm, mmm

Sometimes, it's hard to see what the future holds

And most times, it feels like a steep climb, and that's alright

There's magic in details, the tender small gestures of love

And the way they all add up

When they ask why I can never explain

But a symphony played when you told me your name

And it sounded like a sign

Will you be my beginning, my middle, my end?

Will you be my beginning, my middle, my end?

Will you be my beginning, my middle, my end?

Will you be mine?

Five years later and I'm still yours

Ten years later and I'm still yours

Fifty years later and I'm still your beginning and middle and end

Five years later and I'm still yours

Ten years later and I'm still yours

Fifty years later, and I'm still your beginning and middle and end

Beginning and middle and end (oh)

Will you be my beginning, my middle, my end? (Oh)

Will you be my beginning, my middle, my end? (Oh)

Will you be my beginning, my middle, my end? (Oh)

Will you be mine?

Song by Leah Nobel

Write a note to yourself......

147